ANOINTED LIES

BY

DR. RODNEY E WILLIAMS

ZERAPHATH PUBLICATION

TABLE OF CONTENTS

PREFACE

The multifaceted ways which God use to birth his will into the earth-realm are so vast that we would never calculate them in our lifetime. Sometimes he uses people, sometimes he uses things and sometimes he uses behaviors. Whichever way God choose it is always amazing to us because we never saw the end of the story from our view or viewpoint. Yet there are things which God use that if it were used to bring about a result that favored another, we today would call it unfair, or injustice and in some cases downright shameful. However, when you take the investigative analysis of the purpose and the plan of God to bring to pass those things which brings about his perfect will you would have to look at how he uses the perfect methodology for the perfect moment to bring to pass his will which we call; perfect. This book will bring to light many things, and it will also bring to light the many ways that God use the mind, mouth and motives of others to bring to pass something that was not a perfect plan, but it was the perfect plan for that particular moment. Everybody and everything can and will be used in the plan of God. Every scheme, every plot every plan, every pit and pitfall shall be used in God's plan. This book will bring to the forefront the things which the bible record that we perhaps call sin, Satan and in some cases down right low-down, yet it was used for the glory of God and to bring his people ultimate victory.

CHAPTER 1

HOLY PLANS IN HELLISH PLACES

"How" has become one of the most used words which fall from our lips in these last and evil days? With so many pits, pitfalls, setups, and setbacks, we sometimes ask how God is going to bring to pass this enormous vision that you and I possess. So many times, we've fallen into places of condemnation, and, for one reason or another, we wonder, will we ever arise from this unplanned pitfall? Yet, because God is a God who can see better in the dark than he can in the light, we are never without a way out. Our lives are placed in the hands of God, who operates by providence rather than luck, happenstance, or chance. Whatever happens, God will open the next door even if someone has run off with the keys.

Providence moves us into a place where God wants us to see him for who he is and to see people for who they are not. If God is not with you, you can have everything and everybody it takes to get a job finished, and yet you could never complete it. On the flip side, if he is with you, you can have nothing, no skills nor degree to do what you are attempting, yet God will send the people you need to finish what you need to accomplish. Providence has always existed and has always been in operation, yet we didn't know what it was. Some call it luck; some call it a chance, some say something told me. However, when you realize that God is working from the top, at the bottom, and in the middle, you realize it's a divine arrangement. Though it doesn't make sense yet, it is the hand of the only one who controls things that seem to have fallen apart into a zillion-piece conundrum.

I have discovered that the bigger the question mark, the greater the plot of the story. Yet God will place us around people who are filled with questions. How are you planning to do this? How are you going to meet deadlines? Do you realize you are over budget? Do you realize these people are against your project expansion? Questions that have no answers from humanistic reasoning, yet they have already been answered by the God who makes all things beautiful in his own time. I have discovered that when we attempt something that has no earthly instructions, we have no earthly obstructions because the answers are born from above. *Whatsoever is born of God overcometh the world; and this is the victory that overcometh the world, even our faith. I John 4:4 KJV*

The system that is over our head is not the system that instructs us when people feel that we are over our head. The more we walk with God, the more we rely on him. Even when we can't see the road, we trust the leading of God who brings his children through the Red Sea and over hills and mountains. I have found that the more we rely on him, the more it brings him honor and glory. *This is the confidence that we have in him that if we ask anything according to his will, he hears us and we know that we have the petition wherewith we have asked of him. I John 5:14 KJV* God is sending answers to us even in places where we feel we should not be in the first place. He is sending answers to us when we feel that we have been disenfranchised by others who should have treated us better or been there for us.

The story of Joseph is one of the most interesting stories in the Bible. It is a story that proves you can be hated for no reason, disliked, and even sabotaged by those who are closest to you. Unfortunately, some of these behaviors are sometimes found in our family makeup and structures. However, it is Jesus that said; *"a man's foes shall be those of his own household". Matthew 10:36 KJV.* When we hear these words spoken, we probably say, if I can't count on my family, who can I count on? I know that we are supposed to safeguard one another and be there one for another. However, when we look at many families, we see betrayal and sometimes every evil imaginable, all because someone feels that they should have what someone else has been born with or destined for. Joseph was the son of his father's old age; simply put, he would be considered the baby of the bunch or at least one of them. This was not what placed him in peril, what placed him in peril was the fact that he wore a coat of many colors. This coat represented the favor he had been given by his father.

Many times, we are hated for things that we never looked at as being something that would draw the attention of people or cause people to dislike us. Throughout life, I have seen people who have struggled to be what they are and who they are. Yet because someone felt that the person's success should have gone to them, they do all they can to wreak havoc in the person's life. You can't steal what God has designated to be someone else's. If God has purposed that this success belongs to this young lady, or this success belongs to this man, there is nothing that can be done to stop, block, or destroy the person's level of success. If God has given his word to the person, you can hire a demolition crew and you can't destroy their life. You can hire liars and the lies will work more for their favor than their failure. You can turn people against them that you thought were prominent and were the strength in their structure, only to come out disappointed because God sent someone else to help them.

Joseph is hated by his brothers not just because of the coat, but for the course his life seemingly is taking. He wore his coat, but he told his dreams. When you wear your favor and speak your heart, you will become a target. The reason being is because your prophecy is leaking out of you, and sometimes prophecy leaks prematurely, then sometimes God allows prophecy to leak on purpose. Whatever the case may- be, you are both seen, heard, and you think it's normal, yet it is dangerous if you are in the presence of haters.

The question has to be asked: how do I wear it and hide it at the same time? The truth is there is no way to wear your favor and God's providence for your life and hide it. Favor is too flamboyant to be hidden. God wants us to be humble, but if it's from heaven and God has bestowed it upon us, it can never be hidden from the enemy when he knows what favor looks like. We have all discovered in some way or another that Satan knows what the favor of God is because he had it upon him at one time. This is why those who are chosen have the biggest attacks against them when they move to the next level of vision. Favor is the access code that opens doors when you don't have the key. Favor is what is necessary to keep you alive in hostile situations. When we are favored by God, we are also the target of ridicule and scrutiny. The more the favor in your life, the more you will be defamed, sabotaged, and discussed negatively.

RELATIONAL IMPLOSION

I have discovered that if I am going to cook in the kitchen, I need to get used to the heat from the fire. In order for someone to be a good cook, they can't be afraid of fire, and neither can they let an accidental or incidental burn halt them from preparing the most scrumptious meal they have ever prepared. If you and I are going to go into the destiny in which God has ordained for us, we must realize that there are some things that come along with the territory. One of the many things that come along with being elevated is inside demonic attack. The difference between the words implosion and explosion is that one of them happens from the inside, while another happens from the outside. The number one attack against most individuals will come from *relational implosion*. This means that someone you are related to, someone in your family matrix and structure, attempts to destroy you, and they do it with perfect plan precision because of where they are positioned in your life. Jesus himself stated this and again I will repeat it *"a man's foes shall be those of his own household"*. *(Matthew 10:36)*

The question is asked so many times how can someone close to you be that cruel to you? How can someone who has your DNA not have good intentions for you? One of the devil's main weapons of attack is he will use someone you trust, someone you love, someone whom you have always been there for to attack you. Many times, the element that starts it all is some people have personal issues with themselves which they have never resolved and they allow it to fester and turn into full-blown jealousy. Jealousy is self-poisoning if it's not eradicated or extricated. Then it can be something as common as a material item and an individual may feel your possessions should belong to them. For example, many times I have discounted something that I had, while others saw it as everything.

When you are born with the glory and favor of God upon you, you wear it naturally because you have never been without it. Therefore, everything that comes along with having God's approval upon your life, you have always had. Yet there are some people who will look at you and despise your very presence because you have something that they want, although they don't realize what you have was given to you; not obtained by you. God is not an unjust God, he is fair, and he is unbiased. He lets it rain on the just as well as the unjust. (Matthew 5:45 KJV) However, there are some that believe there is some kind of secret that God has given to some and withheld from others. They seem to believe that God has given something to someone else that he has not given to another.

Every person that is born will begin this life the same way, whether financial status, culture, ethnicity, or skin tone, everyone

6

begins life the same way; *with a breath and heartbeat.* How we embrace the gratefulness of being born is how we challenge life after we are born. Life is a challenge that must be met in order for it to be fulfilling. When we add the fact that God sends us to places for people, and they reject us, it is sometimes a challenge that everyone can't handle. For example, Joseph doesn't understand the level of jealousy that his brothers have for him and consequently he is unaware of the danger in which he is in when it comes to their evil will.

Many of those who are the closest to us have seen the progress that we have made while walking with God and while some can handle it, there are some who can't fathom the thought of it. There are some people who regress rather than progress because they want to please those who are dissatisfied with their success. No person should ever get upset with the progress of another, especially those who are within the family paradigm.

After all, we are all born to succeed. God never made anyone a failure. He made everyone with the same opportunities as everyone else has. Still, because there are some who are not willing to persevere through the hardships and hard times as some others, they plan to destroy the individual who overcomes the challenges that can sometimes hinder success. Success is never given to anyone; everyone must be willing to participate in their own success. Joseph doesn't have a clue about the depths of his brother's jealousy as he continues normal conversations regarding what he has upon him. The most amazing part of his dream is that it had not been manifested, nor had it come to pass. It was futuristic, and it was mystical in its presentation, yet it was intriguing.

Genesis 37:1-8

And Jacob dwelt in the land wherein his father was a stranger, in the land of Canaan. *

These are the generations of Jacob. Joseph, being seventeen years old, was feeding the flock with his brethren: and the lad was with the sons of Bilhah, and with the sons of Zilpah, his father's wives: and Joseph brought unto his father their evil report.

Now Israel loved Joseph more than all his children because he was the son of his old age and he made him a coat of many colors.

And when his brethren saw that their father loved him more than all his brethren, they hated him, and could not speak peaceably unto him.

And Joseph dreamed a dream, and he told it to his brethren: and they hated him yet the more.

And he said unto them, Hear, I pray you, this dream which I have dreamed:

For behold, we were binding sheaves in the field, and, lo, my sheaf arose, and also stood upright; and, behold, your sheaves stood round about, and made obeisance to my sheaf.

And his brethren said to him, Shalt thou indeed reign over us? Or shalt thou indeed have dominion over us? And they hated him yet the more for his dreams, and for his words.

There are some individuals who can't stomach the idea of you gaining or increasing your current elevation. Some can't imagine you acquiring more than what you already possess. It is colloquial to someone having ten of what someone else doesn't have one of, and yet they want five more. Just the very idea of Joseph wearing anything else, atop of the favor he already possesses, just caused his brothers to hate him all the more for his dreams and for his words. Words are the tools that turn any vision into a reality. Words are the invisible materialization of every idea, vision, and dream. When a person dreams and begins to talk about the dreams and visions which they have, it reveals to those listening, the mind of the dreamer, or visionary. If you can't talk about it, you can't walk in it. If you can't voice it, you can't conquer it, it has to be spoken by you. That is the first step of the completion of any vision; open---your----mouth and talk about it!

It will upset some, it will invite some and it will dismiss some, but yet you have to introduce your vision to the outside world. ***Relational Implosion*** is something that must happen. It is the fuel for the future of the survival of one's existence. If there is no one fighting you, then what you are doing isn't born of God. If there is a fight going on, it is a signal that what you have been given is born of God. *I John 5:4 KJV For, whatsoever is born of God overcometh the world: and this is the victory that overcometh the world, even our faith.* Your outside fight is because of an inside revelation. Every great move of God in the earth-realm starts with someone who is willing to defy what everyone else says and go with what God has said to them. It is dangerous, but it's God! I say that it is dangerous because it will draw out every behavior that someone has secretly in their heart. It will show you the true feelings of individuals whom you thought wanted you to succeed just as much as you wanted success.

Joseph, speaking about what he said to his brothers, revealed a level of **relational implosion** that would startle the average. However, when he spoke of his second dream, it revealed something more in-depth than what he had shared with his brothers. God using one person to save the lives of many people is his way of proving that his power is not in numbers, his power is in his nomination. If God nominates you for a specific work, the work will be completed because *he is the God who makes all things work out after the council of his own will. (Ephesians 11:1 KJV)* Joseph's dreams spanned further than just his brothers. He had another dream that was symbolic, yet direct. The symbolism which was revealed in his second dream did not merit him to mention who was included, nor did he have to call names. The dream just spoke for itself.

Genesis 37:9-11

And he dreamed yet another dream and told it to his brethren and said, Behold, I have dreamed a dream more; and, behold, the sun and the moon and the eleven stars made obeisance to me.

And he told it to his father, and to his brethren: and his father rebuked him, and said unto him, What is this dream that thou has dreamed? Shall I and thy mother and thy brethren indeed come to bow down ourselves to thee to the earth?

And his brethren envied him; but his father observed the saying.

Joseph shared his dreams, and he never called names, yet it angered his father to the point that he chastised him concerning the dream which he had. There is something that is going on in the spirit realm at all times, whether you are sleeping or whether you are awake. There is always activity going on in the spirit realm. Joseph is only repeating a message that he had received from another place about a coming time that was futuristic. It wasn't disrespectful, it wasn't to shame or defame anyone, it was to let them know what he had seen, it was from God. However, it is hard to sometimes receive something from someone who is younger than you, or less experienced than those they are speaking to.

For some reason or another, we believe in this world that everything is done by seniority, just in case if someone hasn't told you, God is the God of both priority, and seniority! He has a plan; he has an intent and he is concerned that his people come through whatever they are facing; alive! That is his priority! However, because Joseph was the inexperienced one, and the youngest one; what he was speaking at that time didn't have any clout, nor did it carry any weight. There are many lessons that I learn from Joseph, one of the lessons which stand paramount is his ability to handle ridicule from those in his family. Many times, the ridicule that comes from within our families paralyzes us from going further. The **Relational Implosion** which he faced seemingly was the confirmation of what he saw. There will be times that God mandates that you share what you have seen in dreams and visions, but be well aware of ***Relational Implosion*** that will come from some who may feel that it isn't God because it didn't come from their mouths.

THE CONNECTING PLACE

When God reveals our aspirations and inspirations, we sometimes overlook it within ourselves and we feel that it may or may not be relevant. We judge relevancy by our prayer life and our prophecy. If we have been praying for this to come to pass in our lives or if we have stood before the prophet and the prophet has spoken to us that something is coming to us, we look for it. However, many times God goes around your prayers and prophecy to reveal to you something that you haven't prayed for; nor has it been prophesied to you. When your dreams or visions will bless you alone and a few people around you, it might be something you prayed for or something that you desired. At times, God will send a confirmation through the prophet to tell you, you are on course. However, if you have been chosen by God, get ready to receive something you didn't pray for!

Joseph is the free-spirited choice of a sovereign God. He doesn't have any idea what he has been chosen for. After all, he didn't volunteer for anything. The lot hasn't been cast before him, nor is he of any priestly order. He is just his father's baby son whom he has made a coat of many colors. However, that isn't it, it's more than that. Those who God will use the most are those who did not volunteer, those who are not looking for any position, those who don't care about being seen, praised, or heard. If you are any of what

I just described, you stand a better chance of being used by God than anyone else. This is the season that God is using those "who don't want to be used". Let's look at all those who were chosen by God in the scriptures. Every one of them was involuntarily chosen. The only one who volunteered to be used was Jesus Christ. *Hebrews 10:5 KJV Wherefore when he cometh into the world, he saith, Sacrifice and offering thou wouldest not, but a body hast thou prepared me:*

The Connecting Place is the place where God starts the initial motorization of his plans. Strange as it may seem, he starts his plans in normal places, yet with abnormal abstracts. This means that though it seems to be abnormal, he will extract certain things from a situation that seems to be normal, in order to bring his chosen vessel to the place he needs them to be. Joseph's father sends him to check on his brethren to see how they are faring with their father's sheep. That's a normal thing to do. Everyone had sheep, and the sheep had to be attended to, it's normal. However, his father, Jacob, gave him specific instructions about where they were. They were in Shechem, that's normal. (Genesis 37:1-17 KJV) When Joseph gets to Shechem, they are not there, that's abnormal. When you arrive in the providential place in which God has a purpose for your life, a few things may not be aligned. It will be those crooks, turns, and setbacks that will set the stage in your *Connecting Place.*

Joseph follows his father's instructions, he goes to Shechem, but his brothers aren't there. He searches for them, however, he could not find them, yet he looks. Destiny sometimes places you in places where things should have been. You can give your all to people sometimes and though you have given them your all, they aren't there for you in your most vulnerable time. Sometimes, even with children, parents who gave their all for their children's success end up in nursing homes forgotten by the children they worked so hard for. We are sometimes led to empty places, but for many of us, it is the place where our destiny lies, it's our *Connecting Place*.

Shechem means shoulder.

Shoulder: (1) the part of each side of the body in humans, at the top of the trunk, extending from each side of the base of the neck to the region where the arm articulates with the trunk.

Shechem is the connecting place. It is to the destiny of Joseph what our shoulder is to our body. Just as our shoulder connects us to our other body parts for activity, it in-cooperates our body's functions. There are places in our lives that connect us to the place where God has called us to be. Shechem is the connecting place of Joseph's visions to his destiny. Many times, what God reveals to us in a vision is pretty in presentation, but it has to go through an ugly process. The germination process of a seed is that the seed has to rot in the ground and lose its form in order that it may give way to become another plant and therefore secure its future posterity. In order for Joseph to become to his brothers, what he saw in the dream of their sheaves bowing to him meant that he had to go into the ground, but that's the ugly part of his destiny.

The question might be asked, why does there have to be an ugly part to my destiny? After all, God is God, and he has all power in his hands and he is able to do what he wants to do. Why not just let it go smoothly in transition. That is the truth, he can do all things and he could just allow for a smooth transition to take place as we matriculate to the place he wants to use us. However, in order for any product to withstand rigorous use, it will go through and be warranted; it has to be tested. If it is to bear weight, it must be tempered to handle the weight in which it is going to bear and withstand. The person which God will use to help many individuals will be the person who will be misused, lied to, and defamed by others. Most of the time, the ones who will defame them the most will be the very ones that they have been sent to help.

One clear piece of evidence that Shechem is Joseph's connecting place is he gets lost looking for his brethren and someone directs him to where they are. You will not miss your place of destiny, you may be a little late. However, being late doesn't stop the fulfilment of your destiny. Joseph was lost, however-being lost does not constitute that you are too late. There are certain things that happen along our way that are just too much of a coincidence to be an accident. Have you ever had something happen to you or for you; that was aligning you for something else that would be greater later; yet at the time that it happened, it didn't match what you were doing? Getting lost in a field looking for my brothers who don't even like me. How will this help me? Some would have said I am going home. They don't care for me anyway, and I will just tell my father that I couldn't find them. However, there was something that was in him that caused him to keep looking for his brothers. Why; because destiny calls you sometimes through people who don't even like you!

CHAPTER 2

"IT WILL COME TOGETHER IN SHECHEM BUT IT WILL ALL COME OUT IN DOTHAN."

I have discovered that every interval of life is important if you are seeking God's purpose. His purpose is the fuel for our future. We are never in a place of derision regarding decisions because even our stops, stays, and delays will unfold as divine providence when we complete our assignments. Joseph is happy, he is the typical teenager who is just in that innocent mindset. Many times, we are a target for enemy attacks, but we don't know it. Young, eager and energetic, just trying to find your way through life. Your excitement to someone who has ruined their lives can incite something in that person that you have no clue of. Your bright eyes are open to your future, but someone else's future has been ruined because of the decisions they made. Then sometimes it's just your words, the fact that you have the nerve enough to open your mouth about your next season when others are stuck seemingly in the winter of life.

Joseph is carrying out his father's wishes. He simply believes that there is nothing wrong with sharing his dreams. After all, they are only dreams. Your words are a direct link to your heart and your heart's desire. If you are tied to God, it is a direct link to your future and purpose. When we share our hearts with people, it can provoke them to a Godly jealousy or it can provoke them to deadly envy. The dreams which Joseph had shared with his brothers were innocent to him, but to them they were insults. It amazes me that when you speak about your own destiny and what God has shown to you, it's sometimes an insult to someone else. The question that needs to be asked is this God's way of showing me that what he has spoken is directly from him? People are not quick to come against jokesters, but they will fight a visionary with both hands. The very presence of Joseph caused them to be upset with him. They didn't like him going, and they hated him more when they saw him coming. Is it the coat? Is it that they knew he was favored? Is it the dreams of the sheaves; what is it? There are so many dynamics we can sit around and gesticulate regarding why people feel about us the way that they do. Yet the truth is they are not the determining factors whether we complete our mission or not, they are just the indicators that we are headed in the right direction.

When Joseph came to Shechem, he didn't discover where his brothers were located. They were out of place. However; it is strange that they are in a place where their father didn't send them. Many times, there are people that are supposed to help us. They are supposed to be there for us, yet somewhere between the time we start and we finish, they turn because they believe that we intercepted a message that was supposed to be for them. Deliverance must be brought to past by a deliverer, and everyone doesn't have the capability to be selfless. There are those who have been sabotaged and their destinies have been delayed because of self-aggrandizing imposters. People who just wanted to do it, but all for the wrong reasons. Only those who are chosen by God can sew up wounds that were inflicted by people they tried to help, then take their other hand and help the same people that stabbed them the last time.

Everyone cannot handle what comes from the hands of those who they have been sent to help. What someone says about you when you walk up, is still on their mind when you leave. It matters not how fluent the comments and the compliments are while you are in their presence. What they say when you walk up rolls around in their minds when you leave and long after you have gone. Shechem is where it will come together, *the shoulder*, but Dothan is where it will all come out, *law and custom*. Dothan is where his brothers are located. They are filled with hate and envy. Dothan represents a place where every evil intention that your adversary has against you will come out.

Genesis 37:18-20

And when they saw him afar off, even before he came near unto them, they conspired against him to slay him.*

And they said one to another, Behold, this dreamer cometh.

Come now therefore, and let us slay him, and cast him into some pit, and we will say, some evil beast hath devoured him and we shall see what will become of his dreams.

I afore-mentioned that **Dothan** *means law or custom.*

John 1:11-12

He came unto his own, and his own received him not.

But as many as received him to them gave he power to become the sons of God, even to them that believe on his name.

In Christendom, you will find many incidences in which people whom God had chosen to do work were always being martyred. Before your purpose can truly be revealed, you will suffer great attacks from those who don't want you to be anything else but down. There has to be someone from a low place who intends to keep you from moving into your high place before you discover you are supposed to be there; it's the law, and it's the custom of elevation. No person will ever rise to elevation without first being attacked and secondly knowing that the attack will come from someone close enough to you that it will shock you! I am elated and excited to tell you even when it shocks you, don't let it shake you! It is just the way God identifies those who are against you and it is his way that he reveals those he has placed his hands upon.

"JUST BECAUSE YOU DON'T MEET THE STANDARDS DOESN'T MEAN THAT YOU CAN CHANGE THE RULES"!

God has given unto us all things that pertain to life and Godliness. (II Peter 1:3 KJV) God has given everyone the opportunity to succeed with what they have been given. Whether it's athletic ability, social-economic skills, or an invention, there is no individual who doesn't have the fingerprint of God upon their life. He is just, and he is fair. Joseph's brothers, for some reason, are another felt that they have been dealt with a hand that isn't fair. They feel that they haven't been given what he has been given. Is it the coat? Is it the fact that he was one of his father's youngest children, or is it that he has something that shines brighter than the coat he is wearing? Sometimes you think it's what you drive or where you live, yet that is not why you have the fight that you are having. The truth is, there is something radiating from you that you can't hide, nor can you deny.

God placed a light in us which guides us to the place he called us to be and warns others that we are on our way. *"Let your light so shine before men that they may see your good works and glorify your Father, which is in heaven. "(Matthew 5:16 KJV)* The mandate that God has given to you and I doesn't turn off our light, but rather, it brightens it so others may see. Joseph has to come to the place where his light has blinded the eyes of his brothers to the fact that he doesn't have any ill will against them. Yet because they are filled with envy and jealousy, they couldn't see anything but him being evil. One person being jealous is one thing, but a whole family being jealous is something totally different. Why? It is because there is a standard that God sets inside of every person which he will use. Th*at standard is holiness and sanctification.*

It is what sets you apart from anybody else in the arena or paradigm. There are people that have been killed socially, and physically because they set a precedent that no one else was able to set. They walk in a room and you know they are there, not because they said something or had an entourage with them when they came in. You know that they are there because when they came in God's presence came in with them. They sat quietly in the assembly, said amen, waived their hand, gave their offering, and left. Yet it was something about that individual that left an impression. Joseph carries this aura with him, he carries this weight of God's presence and it couldn't be taken away from him, it couldn't be stolen from him. It was more than the coat that he had on it was an invisible mantle which God had laid upon him long before he realized that he possessed it.

When he comes upon his brothers in Dothan, he comes innocently. He didn't come to rub in their face anything about what he'd dreamed, he was done with that. He saw it, he said it, he was rebuked for it and so be it. However, though he is finished with it, God isn't. Though he is through talking about it, God has yet to speak through it. The brothers that he thought were just being themselves were getting more sinister at heart day by day when it came to him. Why? Because the rules of engagement have been set forth to bring to pass what he has dreamed. I need to warn you that when you are on a collision course to your destiny, things around you will begin to happen that you couldn't hire an analyst that's skilled enough to explain to you what is going on. Hands that open doors for you will start to close them in your face. People who were always respectful sometimes become nasty and disrespectful to you. Don't be disturbed. The rules of engagement have been set forth to push you into what you would have never walked into by yourself.

We are all chosen for what is ahead of us, not for what is going on around us. What is going on around us pushes us to embrace what God reveals futuristically. Joseph was chosen for what was coming, not for what was happening at that particular point. At the interval in which he had the dream, there wasn't anything happening around him or his family. However, God never looks at what you have or where you stand today, more than he looks at where you will be tomorrow and what you might have to encounter when tomorrow comes. *Jeremiah 29:11 KJV "For I know the thoughts that I think toward you, thoughts of peace, not of evil to give you an expected end".* If God waited to choose us at the moment of impact, we would be unprepared for the task at hand. The task sometimes takes years of preparation in order for a person to be adequate enough to handle what they have been chosen for. This is the defining reason that Paul the Apostle says *"wait on your ministry". Romans 12:7b KJV*

Maybe if it was Gad or Rueben, or Simeon, they wouldn't have felt the way they felt, however it was Joseph. Many times, if it's our favorite person, they don't really have to have the character to perform the task, but because they are the favorite of some, they will support them all the way to failure. Success without character doesn't exist, because you cannot truly be successful if you don't have character. The problem that they had with Joseph was they didn't possess the qualities, nor could they meet the qualifications that he had, and therefore they wanted to change the rules. Just because someone doesn't meet the qualifications does not mean they can change the rules! Many individuals want the position, but they do not meet the qualifications to carry out the task. Joseph has what it takes, his brothers do not and so they want to strip him of what he has on him and in him.

I want to reveal to you that you are walking in power and authority. What you have that gives you the ability to do what you do is not on you, it's within you. You should be thankful and praise God that the source of your God-given ability is not on you! If it was on you, someone could have long ago come along to steal it. Or better yet, hijacked you incognito and snatched it away from you, and left you bewildered, shaken, and feeling empty. *God has placed his treasure in an earthen vessel that the excellency of the power may be of God and not of us. II Corinthians 4:7 KJV* People who believe that it is an outside work spend a lot of time trying to perfect things from an outward perspective rather than walking in the power which God places on the inside. Outside things are diadems, medallions, relics, and robes; inside things are holiness, sanctification, purity, integrity, and a consecrated life.

The first thing that the brothers thought was, Joseph's attitude is different from the rest of ours, and it's all because of the coat he is wearing. Ever since our father gave him that coat, he's been vaunting himself up and acting like he is more than us. People would rather pick something they can see and give credence to that particular thing rather than yield to the power of God and what they can't see with their natural eye. To give credit to God is to submit to who he has chosen, and that's the real problem. A lack of submission to a chosen leader is sometimes revealed through others by their actions. Their acts of rebellion signify that they do not trust God's leading through whom he has chosen. Remember the statement that was made to Joseph *"are you to reign over us"*? This statement is a statement of mistrust. This statement is a direct link to the heart and how they felt about him being over them.

One of my favorite passages of scripture that I love to read anytime an opportunity of elevation is laid before me is *Psalms 75:6-7 KJV "For promotion cometh neither from the east, nor from the west, nor from the south. But God is the judge. He putteth down one and setteth up another.* Our elevations must be filtered through trust, and those who we will help must trust the leading of the same God who chose us to lead. Because you don't like God's choice, it doesn't give you the right to override the choice of God by sabotaging who he chooses. There are some that might be reading this and you fit into the genre of being chosen by God and yet unaccepted. You are fought, defamed, disrespected, and misused, and might I add; ***"chosen."***

Never change your status to be accepted in someone's circle when they know beyond a shadow of doubt that God has chosen you. Just because they can't meet the qualifications, don't let them change the rules, and cause you to acclimate to them. After all, they do not have the directions to navigate those who are under the looming threat of demonic attack and generational extinction; but the chosen does! The question needs to be asked: why would you steal something that you can't operate? The next question would be why would you sabotage someone who has the ability to operate it; because it is their ability through God that is going to save your life and the lives of many others.

"IT'S MY DESTINY NOT MY DESTRUCTION"!

One push from the wrong hand can put you in the right place! Many times, the evil intentions of others have caused some to find the place they never would've found, had it not been for the evil intentions someone had against them. Sometimes you become the recipient of ***unintentional elevation***, which means they wished they could take back what they did to you because it was their act that started this all. If there was an award given on a national stage called the Unintentional Elevation Award, you would be shocked by the recipients of it. There would be people from all walks of life, all creeds and nationalities, walking the stage to receive it. The truth is, every person that God has destined to be a deliverer will make their arrival. However, he didn't say how we would get there.

Many of us will have strange travel plans and an unusual itinerary. Some of us will have strange packaging, with beautiful wrapping paper and when it is unwrapped it is a casket, but we will step out of it alive. I have never been disappointed by a sabotage, but I have been disappointed by the person whom it came through. The reason I have never been disappointed by the sabotage itself is because sabotage is the transportation God uses to deliver to his children the things which he has for them. The chaos that you are experiencing is actually a courier, delivering you to a season you have been waiting on, that you could not have walked upon yourself.

Joseph doesn't know the intentions of his brothers, neither does he know the intentions of God, yet he does know he has seen two unusual dreams. Just the mere fact that God has rolled back the curtains of eternity and revealed to you that he has planned for the future makes you stand at attention. Just the fact that I am included in what he is going to do is awe-striking! Though it is awe-striking, it has some deadly consequences attached to it. What Joseph spoke to his brothers and his father regarding his dreams has created within his brothers insidious, malicious hate for him. When his intentions are pure, yet their intentions are the direct opposite, they can't see anything but them bowing to him and him standing over them.

Genesis 37:18-20 KJV

And when they saw him afar off, even before he came near unto them, they conspired against him to slay him. *

And they said one to another, Behold this dreamer cometh.

Come now, therefore, and let us slay him, and cast him into some pit, and we will say, some evil beast hath devoured him: and we shall see what will become of his dreams.

One of the saddest points that you will ever come to in life, is when you see the evil intentions that were planned for you, and the degree of treachery which went into it. It's so sad because you would have never done to the person what they did to you. This is the most paralyzing part of any attack. When you come to the place where you get the chance to see the heart of the person revealed in the action that they perform against you, if you aren't careful, it will make you lose trust in people. The only way you can keep going is that you know that the attack will not outweigh the elevation. God always makes the elevation more attractive than the attack. This means that every time we are attacked by evil, we can expect God to send us elevation. The Word says *had they known what they were doing, they would not have crucified the Lord of glory.* (I Corinthians 2:8c KJV)

The plans that Josephs' brothers had for him were so sinister that one would never think of doing to another human what they planned to do to him unless the plan was from a heart that is black with jealousy and evil. When people see you as someone who is far beyond their reach, their intentions are to get you lower than they are. In Joseph's case, his brothers dug a pit for him. A low place, a place where no one would see you unless they walked up and looked down on you. That is where the enemy wants you and me. He wants us in a pit. He wants us in a place where he is able to walk down and look at us, a place where we are not able to crawl out, a place where we will remain.

What a sad indictment, just because they didn't like your dream, they dug a pit to place you in, just because they didn't like your aspiration and inspiration, they wanted to put you in confinement. Yet you do know that God has plans that include graves, tombs, and pits. Lazarus was in a tomb, yet Jesus called him from his tomb. The lunatic lived in the graveyard and Jesus restored him to a new life in a place of death. Restoration has a reservation for that person that is still in expectation!

I have discovered that the providence of God includes everything your enemy can do, plan to do, and has done to you. The map which leads to your destiny has all kinds of secret codes on it. They include sabotage, frenemies', cousins who had an ill will, individuals who wanted you because they saw in you, an opportunity to stand on your shoulders to get to where they wanted to go. The map to your destiny is laced with people who wanted to make you believe they were doing you a favor when the truth is, the favor that was on your life brought with it all they needed to survive. Yet everything that I have mentioned is not your destruction. It was part of your destiny. It is the very thing that has brought about the attraction to you. However, it will not be the thing that wipes you out.

.

CHAPTER 3

"YOU ARE IN THE WOMB OF PURPOSE; NOT A PIT!"

When God finish using those who are trying to use you, you will see purpose and not people. The people who are against you and even those who are for you will reveal the purpose God has for you. The ministry of purpose is bigger than anything or anybody. It is the reason you survived things that would have killed others. The very thing that is seemingly sucking the life out of you right now is breathing breath into you. There is an adverse effect to everything that happens to us in this life. Sometimes, instead of someone dying from something horrific, they say to themselves, "you will not die from this, calm down. You shall live to see the purpose behind this attack". An adverse effect simply means that something went the opposite of the way that it was originally planned.

At first conception fear sometimes tries to arise and take over, fear is a normal human reaction. However, it will totally shut down your faith if you allow it to remain. There are those who will tell you they have to close their eyes and focus beyond what they were experiencing at that particular time. I have been there myself, I had to get in my mind another view of where I was supposed to be and how life was supposed to be for me. Many times, the people who need you the most are those who respect you the least. That doesn't mean that you are not respectful, or that God has not chosen you. In all actuality, their behavior is what proves that you have been called by God. Josephs' dreams were seemingly disrespectful to those who he told them to because of his position in the family. For some reason, it seemed that he was too young to dream, or he was not old enough to speak into the future of those who were older than he was.

I need to pause here and tell you it is never too early, nor is it ever too late to dream! Never let someone give you permission to dream and never let someone prevent you from repeating what God has shown you. Joseph's only infraction is that he had the audacity to open his mouth and say what he saw. When we look at where he's placed because of his favor, it shouldn't make us scared to wear our coat, it should cause us to be aware that everyone isn't happy because you see something better. The truth is, there is no way around the treachery that others have for you when they see your purpose. This pit that his brothers have dug for him is supposed to be the place that tames him and puts him back in his place. However, they are sadly mistaken. The pit which they have placed him in is actually *the womb of his purpose*. It will be the place from which his destiny will be birthed, and it all will come from the hands of someone who thinks they are doing him evil.

Womb: the organ in the lower body of a woman or female where offspring are conceived and in which they gestate before birth. The place where an unborn fetus develops and grows.

32

A pit is a low place, Joseph is caught and thrown down into this pit, but what he doesn't know is his destiny had conceived him, and what he doesn't realize is from this pit he will be birthed into what God had planned for him. When it is time for a baby to be born, the female's water can break sometimes in an unusual place. It doesn't ask permission, or is it okay to do it here, no it just happens and when it happens everyone makes the adjustments that are necessary for the baby's arrival. Just like a woman whose water has broken; this is how we are pushed into our destiny. No "hey wait a minute", no "hold on I'm not ready just yet," when the time comes it comes without announcement. There are so many people who have been pushed into their destiny by a friendly hand with treacherous intentions.

It was scary, it was painful, but most of all it was necessary because you have to know Joseph is not going to jump into this pit, nor is he going to develop standing around his haters. The pit puts you in the birth canal, while standing around talking to your brothers who don't see what you see or have what you have, does nothing but let you grow in size, but the pit will allow you to grow in size, character and most of all it will push you into your purpose. The very place that we look at as the end for us is the very place that God is saying no, this is the beginning. The next time you're placed somewhere you wouldn't have placed yourself, ask yourself; is this my pit, or is this my birthing place? Is this a womb or is this a tomb? Is this the birth of my destiny? When you ask these questions, you have to start looking around to see what is the catalyst that has started this all. Is it something I said, is it something I have on me that has caused me to be placed where I am?

The questions which come back unanswered are the directives that bring confirmation that you are walking in your destiny. I have questions that can't be answered and the reason that they can't be answered is because the answer is in the future. What we love about serving God is that he will eventually give us the answer to every question that we have, whether it's a fill in the blank, multiple-choice, or essay, God majors in answering questions. With the purpose of your destiny also comes the confirmation of dreams to those who thought you were being subliminally assertive.

Many times, we have seen people who use vision as a way to exalt themselves to others to make them believe that they are super spiritual. However, then there are those that have dreams and visions that are too specific for it not to be God. I have heard dreams from both spheres, dreams from those who conjured up something, and those who had been arrested by destiny. Those who had been arrested by destiny treated the vision like it was a normal day and they would repeat it verbatim if asked by someone.

Joseph is at the zenith of his purpose and none of it was making sense to him. I need to share with you that there is a place where the behavior of those around you will not make sense at all. It is at this place that you have to laughingly view that in the womb the baby doesn't shake hands, nor does it go to birthday parties, nor does it receive invitations to outings. When you are in the womb of your destiny, you will find that you will lose more relationships than you gain. It is the newness of a separation that sometimes makes people miss their purpose. They can't get used to being without someone who they may have thought was supposed to be with them on their entire journey. It can be an emotionally stressful time, and even traumatizing if you don't have a prayer life. God's purpose for us is the reason we are here; I don't have an existence outside of the purpose of God in my life. You and I were not placed here to take up matter and space. We were placed here to carry out another piece of God's plan for someone who may be coming on behind us. If that doesn't take place, we have wasted a lifetime doing nothing but pleasing people and pleasing ourselves.

The question may be asked: how do I get out of the womb of my purpose? Many times, during birth, the mother has to have help to birth the baby. There are various techniques that are used to help push the baby through the birth canal. However, each technique that is used to help the mother is done through the hands of another person. Whether forceps, cesarean session, episiotomy, or just a gentle tug or an encouraging voice that says push, you are almost there. Whatever the methodology used, it comes from someone else. Just like the techniques that I mention come from another person to help the mother birth the baby, in order for the purpose to be birthed, it will come through someone encouraging you or discouraging you.

There will be times that the encouragement of someone who is outside of what you are experiencing, will be exactly what you will need to help push you into becoming what God has called you to be. Then sometimes it's through someone discouraging you, discrediting your work in a negative way. Instead of their negative actions discouraging you, it is what actually pushes you into your purpose. Persecution can be the most welcoming adornment to your purpose. Even though it doesn't make you feel good at that particular time but down the road around the corner, you will look back and say "this was the Lords doing". *It was good that I have been afflicted that I may learn thy statutes. (Psalms 119:71 KJV)*

"YOU WILL KNOW THE PEOPLE WHO ARE STANDING AROUND YOUR PIT!"

Psalms 41:9 KJV "Yea, mine own familiar friend, who I trusted, which did eat of my bread, hath lifted up his heel against me.

If there is any place you can be comfortable at, it would be home and around family members and close friends. At home we feel that we are in a safe environment and when you are in a safe environment, you tend to miss little things that are big things in all actuality, but because of who it came from, you let it pass. Had an outsider said or done some of the things to us that were said by someone we trusted; a red flag would have immediately gone up. Truth and true feelings come through jokes and statements that have smiles behind them. People plant and plan their attacks long before they detonate them.

However, before they execute their plan, they have to infiltrate your life through smiles, gestures and cosmetic kindness. Joseph is in this pit because he had no idea the degree of treachery that lay within his brothers. Being their younger brother, his mentality was probably; "I know they thump my ears and all because they don't like that I am the baby of the family, but that's all they are going to

36

do to me; after all, I am their brother." There are many people who are in the places they are today because they trusted someone they knew so little about, with too much of the intricate parts of their lives.

Joseph's childlike instincts have landed him in a pit. However, that's not the treacherous part. The treacherous part is that he is in this pit because of his own brothers. Can you imagine being stripped of your coat and put in a hole, then looking up only to see the snarl on the faces of those who placed you there? That alone is scary, but to see that though you know them, they are serious! I've played the dozens with my cousins and siblings before, as I am sure that most people have. You start off sometimes playing and it was funny, then you realize that though you started off playing, they had turned serious. There are some people who jest with you and then along the way you see their heart and certain deep-seated behaviors start to come out. Joseph probably thought it was just a little game that they were playing, but after they placed him in the pit and left him there all night, he realized it wasn't a game.

There are many people who have been placed in a hole by deceit, defeat, and ill-willed conceit, and sadly, they know the people who are standing around their pit. The pain that comes from it is one thing, but the long-lasting effects of it is another. You loved them and you invited them into your life or circle with the intent to have a wholesome relationship with them for life, but some individuals do not want *a place*-they want *to replace* you with themselves. The saddest thing is God's visionary for a task is irreplaceable, which means you can't be replaced by an imposter or a counterfeit, you can only be replaced by a successor. Yet, there are some who believe that if I can just get them out of the way, I can take their place.

God protects us by not allowing the ill-willed plans of people to come to pass, and we never go through what they have planned, and therefore we never see who is behind it all. Then there are times that he shows us the faces of those who are standing around *our pit*. Imagine looking up and seeing all your brothers looking down at you and none of them having enough nerve to tell the others; enough is enough. We have all wished that we had someone to fight for us and ward off the evil attacks which were coming against us. However, when it is from those who are family, people figure that it is a harmless game of family rivalry. Therefore, those who have your back, stay away and say it will all end at a picnic, but not in Joseph's case. It ended with him in a pit!

Genesis 37:22 KJV "And Reuben said unto them, Shed no blood. Throw him into this pit that is in the wilderness, and lay no hand upon him; that he might rid him out of their hands, to deliver him to his father again."

Though it seems like heinous maliciousness and evil, when God gets ready to operate in us and through us, he prepares us to handle what we have been sent to accomplish. The preparation to outsiders looks like punishment, but it's not punishment, it's preparation; no preparation for what is ahead of us would be punishment. We must realize that in order to survive what is ahead of us, the preparation must be on the same level as the attack or greater if we are to survive the road ahead.

Many times, children feel that parents are mean when they are rearing them. However, it is only after they become grown that one day, they say to the parents that they thought was so mean "thank you". if you had not prepared me with the kind of training I received, I wouldn't have been able to survive. The world is not kind, especially to those who have been sent by God to take his people from darkness. I have seen many times unprepared people taken advantage of because they had no preparation. No preparation makes you vulnerable to those who prey on people who haven't been trained to see predators.

I report sadly to you that the best training you will ever receive for what is ahead is from those who are the closest around you, those who you thought would protect and cover you. Joseph has been prepared for his purpose by and through the hands of his brothers. Not just his brothers, but you have to remember the rebuke of his father as well. I want to speak to the individual who is doing all they can do seemingly and for some reason, you are always being ridiculed, pushed around, and every time you say something, it is disavowed as nothing. There are times that confirmation comes as a rebuke, then there are times that it comes in the form of people not wanting to hear anything you said, saw, or felt. It is at this point that you will either yield to them; or you will muster up the strength to press on.

The pain of knowing the faces of those who stand around your pit must be turned into the power that will help you live through it. I have been hurt many times by the fact that it was those that I helped to be where they were that turned to be my worst enemy. I empowered my ditch diggers; I gave my adversary an opportunity and they stood and railed on me. It is what happens when you are the only one in the room who isn't jealous of anybody. When you are the one who wants to see everyone blessed, and everyone successful, get ready for the pit, but also don't be shocked by who is behind you being placed in it! It will be those with whom you shared your vision with, those who you left a rock in the door for, so when they came, they could get in places that you already had favor in.

The pit is a five-star hotel for you. What? Yes, I said it. The pit is a five-star hotel for you. It is the place where you will see the luxury of being empowered enough by God to last through the night. It is a place where you will wash out of your mind that everybody is for you. It is the place that when you come out of it, you will have a fresh mind and you will know who is against you, and you will start to look for who is for you. Geographical position doesn't stop prophetic positioning, it only magnifies your prophecy. For someone to do everything that they can to you and against you and you still make your providential arrival, says something. It says God uses many attacks as attachments to the message he has given us about our destiny.

When you receive an email with an attachment to it, an extra action has to be performed in order for the attachment to be viewed. Disliking Joseph is one thing, but taking the time to methodically place him in a hole is extra! The question is "Lord, why are my enemies so extra when it comes to my arrival to what you have promised me"? The extra steps which people sometimes go through to prevent others from what God has spoken to them are sometimes the very reason they press on after the attack. Those standing around the pit they dug for you prove that they have a great fear that what you said you saw; you did see it. Familiar faces behind the attacks which come against you corroborate the vision which God has shown unto you.

"Your enemy's place in your prophecy is just as important as the prophecy itself. Their place in your prophecy secures your place in the outcome of your prophecy."

Rodney E. Williams

"YOU DON'T HAVE TO LIE ABOUT IT!"

We have all seen people commit heinous crimes that are open and shut cases, yet they go and hire high-profile lawyers to try and persuade the jurors that the video footage is a hoax, and their eyes are really not seeing what they are viewing. I have always been of the persuasion that if you are bold enough to commit the offense, wait for the authorities. Joseph's brothers stripping him of his coat and throwing him into a hole is evil, and it was an atrocious act. However, there is another act that was more heinous and insidious than that, that act is that they went home and lied to their father about what happened to their brother.

Never allow what people say to blind or mislead you and cause you to disregard what they aren't saying! There are many people who have lost their lives because of someone who decided that they would only tell pieces of a story, rather than laying the whole truth on the line and allowing it to be revealed. Life should not be lived under the shadows of lies and twisted half-told stories. When the truth is not told, judgment is perverted. Not only is judgment perverted and thwarted, but choices are also made that ruin good people, it throws off and slows down the fulfillment of destiny for others. Not only that, but it allows for witches and warlocks to slide into places which they would never have been able to procure without the lies. There are imposters in positions because they lied to be there. Then there are people who are married and their entire marriage is on a fragile foundation because, if the truth be told, lies drafted them as a bride or a groom. A falsity helped to sway their minds to believe that this is the person for me, all the while they have been duped with lies.

There is an old saying that states, honesty is the best policy, but actually honesty is the only policy! When someone asks for the truth with something that is as serious as the rest of their life, the responding party has a responsibility to provide the truth. If the truth is placed on the table, then if the person makes the choice with the truth being revealed, righteousness has arisen. This is the hour of deception. This is the time that Satan has laid the groundwork for deceptive onslaughts to be placed in the way of the children of God, in order to steal their coat, and kill the calling of those who are chosen by God. There is no such thing as a little white lie, a lie is a lie, and it can have deadly consequences.

Joseph's brothers are lying to their father because they know and believe that there is something to the dreams which Joseph has had. However, they are so blind by envy and jealousy that they totally looked past the fact that they were included in the dreams he described to them. Maybe it was where they were located in the dream that made them feel like they felt and acted in the manner in which they behaved. They were bowing, he was standing, at least they were alive. Many times, your position draws all types of people to you. They will come from all walks of life, some from other states, some from other regions, countries and sometimes it will draw demons straight from the pit of Hell! Positions draw people who wish to be helped, strengthened, and empowered, then there are times when position draws people who wish to do nothing but make sure that they destroy everything in their path.

Joseph's brothers saw an opportunity to stop what they knew to be something beyond their ability to control, that something was providence. They knew that he was on a collision course with something that would give him a reigning position over them. I want to say that when you have it, those around you will tell you, by how they treat you. There are places on the way to your destiny that you will have to read signs along the way, then there are places where you will have to read people. Most of the time when we come through something, we are so overjoyed about it that we sometimes forget the lessons that we were taught in it. God can bless you so good coming out that you forget the agonizing days you spent in the midst of your trial. Yet we will never forget the lessons that we learned while we were going through the trials that we suffered.

The treachery of the lie that was told to Jacob is so heinous because it leads him to believe that his son is dead and that his favor can be killed. However, the blood on Joseph's coat is symbolic of Jesus's blood being upon the favor of each person God has his hands on. You can't remove favor with lies, and nor can you remove it with the truth. There are some things that we are accused of and it is true, yet human frailty and fleshy weaknesses can't nullify God's divine favor. Joseph's immaturity placed him in peril at the hands of his brothers. His innocent eyes and his child-like trusting nature are what prevented him from seeing that his brother's intentions were deadly.

There are times that we were blind and walked into the trap that our enemies set for us. It was just a case of mistaken identity. God has the ability to take the greatest attack that you have ever suffered and use it as the greatest witnessing tool in your evangelistic arsenal. It isn't the attack that sometimes paralyzes us. It is the methodical trickery and the lies that were told on the way, that just almost zaps the life out of you when the attack is revealed.

Never underestimate the jokes and the laughs that come with the sarcasm that individuals use as softening blows. Long before you are attacked, there will be small things that will be said, little innuendos dropped here and there, just to see how you respond to what is said. The most direct message you can receive from people is how they respond when you say something about promotion or elevation. There is an ungated, uncontrollable response that will come from those who sit in the shadows when you speak of your elevation. However, because Joseph didn't have the eyes of wisdom, he never detected his brother's serious intentions to destroy him.

Then there is another dynamic which I would like to reveal, and that dynamic is do you really care how people will respond, knowing that if God is for you, they can't stop you anyway. There is a playful spiritual confirmation, that causes us to laugh at those who are frowning and grimacing at us, as we move toward the fulfilment of our destiny. I have many times have had to turn what I was facing into a game of checkers; I make my move and then they make theirs. All the while knowing that God is sooner or later going to make his move. If you take the offense personally, it will alter your personality, and you will become someone who you don't even recognize anymore. I'm not telling you too not be vigilant and watchful. I am telling you, that just as you include prophecy as confirmation, be sure that you add the subtle words that others say to you, camouflaged in the form of jokes; for that too is confirmation.

CHAPTER 4

"THE FIRST LIE EVER TOLD"

There are times we look and think about the many things we read in the paper or we see on television. Some of it is fictional, then some of it is a live account of someone's actions. The stories which are made up, we look at them and say they are fiction. Yet there are stories we hear concerning others who have moved the lines of the truth for situations to work out for their good. Yet we go about each day saying I wonder why they did that or why did this have to come about this way. When we look at the world around us, it is made up of all kinds of systems as well as secret societies which we are not supposed to know of or about. It is filled with people who have made commitments to organizations to uphold the code of secrecy at all costs.

These individuals are dead set upon keeping their commitments to their organizations so that they can keep their place in society or in the eyes of those who feel and believe that they are in the elite class. They live in a neighborhood which is gated and guarded. They have the biggest house on the street. Their children go to the finest schools. However, when you investigate the premise upon which they stand, you find out that their whole lives are built upon a lie, which is covered by another lie. Their job is a front, their tax returns are fraudulent, yet it is perpetuated through generations and kept floating because the lie works. Why? It works because everybody keeps the lie in the same consistent groove which it has always traveled.

We have said that God will separate right from wrong. We have made consistent testimonies that the wicked will not win, or they will not succeed in their efforts to do what they are doing. Yet when we watch them over and over again prosper in their wickedness, if we are not careful, we will become indoctrinated with the condescending ideology that wickedness always prevails. Time and time again, the news reveals the blatant evil which happens in the world which we live in: and how each and every day someone who is guilty walks out of court because the law has been written with loopholes and codes within it. This reveals that if you can find the right high-priced lawyer who went to the right law school and has an age-old affinity with the judge, not to mention his family, you walk out a free individual. Is that right? No, it isn't right, but it is the layout of the system. The ugly truth is that the justice system is built on an ugly lie dressed in pretty terminology. No individual who lives in America who has watched the evils unfold can say that the system is just. No individual who is a minority can say that they have been treated with equal treatment according to the law. No individual who is of the majority can say that they have not been given "privilege" because they are the majority.

The age-old trickery which has been used to play one of us against the other is the oldest trick known in the history of man and mankind. The belief that one of us is better than the other, or that one of us has more value than the other, is the very core of the evil in which we see boiling in this world today. When one person feels that he is superior to another, you will always have a false narrative and therefore the underlayment of human existence is in sinking sand.

I cannot be the whole person that God has created me to be if I think the person beside me is only half of what and who I am. *Human Wholeness* consists of unity, respect, and endearment. Human existence must embrace human wholeness for man and mankind to exist in their God-created form. If mankind sees anything other than mankind when we look at another person, we are not seeing creation the way God created it to be. If creation is merchandised for gain because I see you as inferior to me because of your skin, sin, or status in the financial tier, I have altered God's creation and have made myself an idol.

The first lie that was ever told in the Bible reveals to us that the "I'm better than you are syndrome" was placed in the mind of mankind by Satan. Satan passed his flawed idealism to mankind in order that he would have a second attempt to do what he failed to do in his first one. His first attempt was to take over heaven and to demote God from being God and destroy the trinity.

Isaiah 14:12-17 KJV

How are thou fallen from heaven, O Lucifer, son of the morning!

How art thou cut down to the ground, which didst weaken the nations!

For thou has said in thine heart, I will ascend into heaven, I will exalt my throne above the stars of God: I will sit also upon the mount of the congregation, in the sides of the north:

I will ascend above the heights of the clouds; I will be like the most-High.

Yet thou shalt be brought down to hell, to the sides of the pit.

That they that see thee shall narrowly look upon thee, an consider, thee, saying, is this the man that made the earth to tremble that did shake kingdoms;

that made the world as a wilderness, and destroyed the cities thereof; that opened not the house of the prisoners?

With this conception and premeditated evil in mind, it reveals to you and I why Satan would attempt to take over heaven. After his failed attempt to carry out his plan in heaven, he is kicked out of heaven and falls into the earth as a fallen reprobate. His intent now is to find an agent who is as rebellious as himself to perform the task which he could not perform. Every evil that you see in the world is because whoever is carrying out that plan is under the influence of satanic powers. Carrying out the attempt to make one believe that he is better than the others and that he has more privilege than another is evil at its finest. I need to tell you that from his original attempt up to this present moment, Satan has made this plan work. So, he is operating at 100% maximum success in doing what he does; and so is God. Many times, we have seen evil side with evil, while the ones who are innocent and walking righteously are ridiculed and heckled for even bringing evil to the forefront. When will justice step from behind injustice and when will righteousness step out of unrighteousness?

That is the age-old question that has been shouted from the crowds of marchers who march across this country. It has been shouted from the steps of courthouses, as some injustice is going on that has been swayed by power, political views, and pedigree. It is one of the most disheartening things to see when someone has their life snatched away from them because one person, for some reason or another, felt that they wanted the spotlight, or felt that they were owed something that they really didn't work for, or that they really don't deserve.

It is hard to even imagine that what we see as a blatant open and shut case can sometimes be appealed and litigated all the way back into legal status through some amendment that favors the side of the guilty rather than the innocent. Many of the injustices that have gone on in this world are because of someone who had the ability to argue their case all the way to the highest court. While others thought the claim was too preposterous to be heard, they with persistence in their heart and with their unrighteous plea in their mouth, pushed forward. We are living in a nation which embraces lies and liars over truth and righteousness. Why? The question must be asked when, and why did things turn to be like they are now? There are so many individuals who have fallen into the altruistic attitude toward truth and what is right and what is just. Jesus said in ***Matthew 24:12 KJV*** *"because iniquity shall abound the love of many shall wax cold."* The question must then be asked: what is iniquity?

Iniquity comes from the Latin, combining the prefix in- "not," and aequus, which means "equal" or "just." So, iniquity literally means ***"not just."*** Iniquity can also be used to say that something lacks moral or spiritual principles.

We look at the world and we see that it has begun to take on the very definition of iniquity. When you investigate the things which we see and look at them closely, you will see that lies are more prevalent than truth in the world's system. When we take a close account, it is easier for a criminal to prove himself innocent than for someone who has been morally sound and lived an upright life. Why? Because iniquity has taken over and has spread itself like a fungus taking over a lush green meadow or yard. Evil unchecked breeds evil uncontrolled. When there is no one to stand and show what is right and invite truth to the platform, the system spins out of control and lawlessness becomes the order of the day. We have become a nation that is ***guided*** by crooked principles but ***guarded*** by a righteous God. Which says that the God which we serve is watching us with a gavel in his hand.

The liars are placed in the right place, the false witnesses take the stand with the check already in their accounts for telling the lies they are about to tell. Tears fall from their eyes like they are playing a starring role to win an Emmy or Tony Award, and right down to the last teardrop they cry and lie. All while some poor individual who was innocent, is heckled as they are led away through a backdoor to escape the massive crowd full of evil hecklers, who are hooked to the vindicated person by the same sin or the under-handed scheme, from which they have just been acquitted of. Everything that we see in our world which goes against the Laws of God can be attributed to the fact that Satan is a liar and the father of all lies.

John 8:44 KJV *"Ye are of your father the devil, and the lusts, of your father ye, will do. He was a murderer from the beginning and abode not in the truth, because there is no truth in him. When he speaketh a lie, he speaketh of his own; for he is a liar, and the father of it."*

Every child will in some way resemble their parents. Sometimes it will look more like one parent than the other, or it will possess a behavior that is more favoring to one parent than the other. Whether by action or physical feature, the child will carry something that ties them to its parents. Jesus brings this vividly clear when he tells the Pharisees you are just like your father, the devil. The lust that you do, you do it because he was the same way. The murders you commit, you commit them because he was a murderer from the beginning and he killed because he would not abide in the truth, simply because there is no truth in him. Then he takes an interesting approach and says that his very nature is to lie, for he is a liar and the father of all lies.

A lie is a tool that Satan uses to destroy people, progress, and promises. Many times, it is the only thing that he can use from his tactics and tricks that will work. Lives have been destroyed because of lies, homes have been wrecked because of them and many people are even sleeping in a cold wet watery grave, all because of a lie. When an individual will say something against someone else and knowingly say something that is not true, it reveals that they are working for Satan. I have witnessed it happen and I am sure that you have as well. When we read the Genesis account of Adam and Eve, we see very clearly their encounter with the devil. They were placed in a Garden that provided them with everything that they would ever need and want. Yet there was something greater than the material things that they had, and it was the presence of God himself.

God's presence always causes the enemy to be attracted to our space. Any person who has the presence of God in his life rests assured that somewhere in proximity, Satan is there. God gave them instructions that every tree in this garden is good for food, but the tree that is in the midst of the garden thou shall not touch, for the day that you touch it your eyes will be opened and you will become as gods (little g). Temptation has always been present in the world. It has always been the downfall of mankind and many times not because of the desire of the thing which is offered, but to see what would happen after the experience. The serpent was the easiest entreating thing in creation. Simply put, the snake was the best avenue to take if you wanted to throw someone off course or out of the will of God. Satan entered the garden through the serpent, and he talked with Eve regarding the forbidden tree. His question was, "Has God said ye shall not eat of every tree of the garden?"

Every question does not deserve an answer, because every question is not appropriate, especially when it questions the sovereignty of God. The question that Satan asked Eve was not just asked, but it was asked in the right way. When a lie is told, if it is mingled with the right amount of truth in it, if you are not careful it will entangle you with curiosity, thus, you end up falling into sin. This is what happened to Eve. The right lie with the right amount of truth caused her to investigate the possibility of being like God. This lie caused her to eat of the forbidden fruit and she then gave it to her husband Adam, and he ate and caused them both expulsion from their creative place. It was the first lie that was ever told in the history of mankind's existence. It was this lie that moved man from his God-given estate and changed the course of God's original plan for man.

"THIS IS THE LAST TIME YOUR ENEMIES WILL PUT THEIR HANDS ON YOU"

There are grave mistakes which Satan has made when it comes to him attacking God's chosen vessels. There are some things which have been the most vital part of solidifying the necessary elements that have pushed so many people into their purpose. There are times we asked ourselves why did God allow me to suffer this at the hands of such evil individuals. Why did he not just lead me around this, or why didn't he just cut this part out of my story, and leave only the good parts that bring me honor and that brings him glory? You also must ask yourself the question: would I go see a movie that doesn't have a plot to it, which will keep me on the edge of my seat? Would

I go see a movie that I could almost figure out what was going to happen before it happened? God wants our story to be more thrilling and chilling than the latest action film. He wants our lives to be decorated with pain, pits, persecutors, and finally, promotion. He uses every bit of what we suffer to make it happen. It doesn't feel good, nor does it always look pretty, but it makes for a real good testimony, and a lot of praise.

Those who are around you follow you more closely than you realize, though they may not talk to you daily, weekly, or ever. There are some people that know more about you than you think they know. There are some who watch you from afar, and then there are some that desire to have what you possess, in a good way. Then you have those who desire what you have, and they will do anything at any cost to make sure that they achieve their goal of obtaining it by any means necessary. We will spend our entire life learning. However, many of the lessons that we have learned left scars on our physical beings. These scars teach us lessons each time we look at them. We are reminded of what not to do again. Just as scars can be left on a person's physical body, they can also be left in one's spirit, emotions, and upon one's conscience.

My physical scars send me messages through my sight, which then return them back to my memory and I remember how and why I have the scar. However, the scars that are embedded in my spirit, or those that are deeply bedded in places that when I come to certain battles again, I am reminded of how I gave too much to the wrong people, too long. When we are faced with something that resembles what has scarred us within our spirit, we apprehensively try to get through this new situation with keen discernment. Many people have been left without the help that they need. Simply because someone was simply afraid to help them for fear that they might be acting a certain way as a ploy, to gain access to them so that they can destroy them with some ungodly attack.

Then there are the scars that are left upon the emotions. Sometimes, after you have poured out your heart and given your all, regardless of how much you did, you yet ended up with nothing but emotional scars. Emotional scars will prevent you from walking into your destiny with open eyes; note I said with open eyes. The scars will not prevent you from walking into your destiny in totality, but they will stop you from enjoying the trip. God wants us to see where we were, and compare it to where he is taking us to. Scars in our emotions stop us from loving again. Divorce is a terrible thing within itself because you end up in a battle with someone you shared your life and heart with. However, to carry the scars that were placed in your emotions throughout your entire life is far worse than being divorced. The judgments of others who stood on the outside and looked in, the ridicule of those who heard the story of the other party, does nothing but add scars, and more scars.

Conscience: *the sense of consciousness of the moral goodness or blameworthiness of one's own conduct, intentions, or character, together with a feeling of obligation to do right or be good.*

Lastly, the scars can be left upon one's conscience. God has given to us conscience to help regulate our actions in this world, as well as our thoughts. When we make decisions, we all want to make the right decisions in life. To make sure that we have a spiritual filtering mechanism, God has given to us our conscience. This is the direct connection we have to the original intent for which God has made us. This is the untainted part of a person and despite how he or she responds, God has given to each person the way they should respond when they filter their response or behavior through their conscience. If you make the wrong response, your conscience causes you to know what response you should have made regarding the decision. It is from the premise of conscience that I say that Joseph's brothers knew that it was wrong to do to him what they did. However, I want you to imagine that though it was their actions; Joseph carried all the scars from their actions.

When you are in the hands of someone who is masterful in taking advantage of people with their manipulative ways, it will cause you to feel that you have done something. Rather than them doing something to you, you see yourself as the cause of everything that has gone on. In some instances, some feel that they provoked the individual to mistreat them and therefore they are in a cage of guilt which they've placed themselves in. Many times, people are scared of life because they can't get over the things which have happened to them. They believe that they could have done something different to affect what happened to them when they didn't actually do anything to cause them to be in their situation.

God wants us to live our lives free and to the fullest. Whatever your gift and your calling is, God entrusted it to you that you could make an impact on the world, that you may empower people to come to their full potential. Even when someone or some group of people try to shortcut you from carrying out that commission, you should arise and command your focus back to your assignment. In order to do that, you must have one important thing in the forefront, and that is "memory". Remembering what God said and what he has shown you will always bring you back to that *fire-place*. Not by the hole in the wall that was built with brick and mortar where you burn wood in the winter. No, the *fire-place* is that place where the fire burned in your heart to fulfill what God had given to you. Many individuals need to return to the *fire-place* in order that they may receive a fresh revelation of their orders from the God of fire.

Where you are located geographically, sometimes may be too small to handle the magnitude of where you are heading. When this happens, you will have attack after attack from people who see you as nothing and nobody, because to them you are normal. They will attack you for your natural state of being. It could be something as simple as the way you talk and how you talk about what God has shown to you. Sometimes it is your standard and how you like things done with kingdom order according to God's standards. Simply put, you can't stop them from attacking you, but God can. When your time comes to go forth and be what God has called you to be, he will begin to use the attacks as transportation to take you to where he will use you the greatest. It is at this point all of your emotions and affinities will have to take a backseat. The reason being is providence works totally through God's will, and not your feelings, nor by your friends. The hands of your adversaries are opening a door for you, but they think it's a pit. Imagine how many emotions would arise within you if someone were to put their hands on you, to push you or shove you as a method to degrade or humiliate you.

People who are kind and not rambunctious are shattered when someone tries to mishandle them in a violent way. However, imagine if it is someone you have a relationship with, they grab your shirt or shove you with ill intentions, when you have no idea what they are doing and why. This is how Joseph must have felt, but what he doesn't know is this is the last time his enemies will put their hands on him. After this attack, they will never be able to attack him anymore, nor will they be able to prevent him from what God is about to do through him. There are many people because of the hands of others and the sabotage that comes from being chosen, who have missed some of the beauty of being hand-picked by God.

I prophesy in the name of Jesus that this is the last time your enemy's hands will be able to touch you. This is the last time their insecurities will be able to infiltrate your confidence. This is the last time their inability to see their own destinies will be able to stifle how you see yours.

"YOU ARE ABOUT TO STEP INTO YOUR DIRTY DESTINY"

There are individuals who have beautiful spotless lives. They were born into a wonderful two-parent home where their mothers and fathers stayed together until one or the other passed away. Because of that example, they were too married and stayed married for years without a flaw. That is wonderful, and we all wished that our lives would mirror the picture perfectness which we see revealed in the lives of others, but everyone's life and the story will not be the same. For some, like myself and many others, they will come from one-parent homes. They will be raised by the hands of a loving mother or father who did the best that they could with the means they had. Then there are those of us who will do all we can for those that we marry and the children we raise, only to see it end in divorce. Relationships that had beautiful starts, sometimes end standing before a judge in front of total strangers.

Truth is that many people will arrive in beautiful places, but they will experience some ugly things along the way. Things that they don't want to talk about, nor do they want to look at the ugliness of its reality. We sometimes end up in places, not by our choice, but we end up there because we are the victim of another's actions. We didn't plan to be where we are. We had made plans to buy land, build a house, and live happily ever after. However, because destiny has many detours, crooks, and turns, we are sometimes tossed into a paradigm that we ask ourselves; just how did I get here? The more you think about where you are and the results of being there, the more you contemplate where this road is leading me to. If God is working all things after the counsel of his own will, it is in his will that I be where I am, though I do not understand the reasoning fully for being here.

The will of a person sometimes has nothing to do with their destiny. I know several people who have spent years preparing for a career by going to college, and once they received their degree, they decided this is not what I want to do. Strikingly, they ended up doing something that didn't even require them to have a degree. Destiny is the events that will unfold for or to a person, things that are out of the person's control. There are things which will happen to you and me which shall be out of our control, though we would choose to believe that we have it under control. I rest in full assurance of knowing that God's providence is always better than my choices. What he predestined for me is always a better plan than my vision board, or my short-term and long-term goals. When God brings you and me to our destiny, though it might be unsightly, unpleasant, and many times unusual, we yet have to say like Jesus in the garden of Gethsemane, *"not my will, but thy will be done";* because that is what is going to take place, whether we like it or not.

I reservedly say that we all have some dirt in our destiny, we all have some spots that we try to wipe down when we give our **"testimony "**. Though it is not a word in the dictionary, I would like to give the word **"des-ti-mony"** a definition. The definition that I would give it is, the things that happened to me which I couldn't control, but after it happened, I was glad that it happened, it was my "destiny and its part of my testimony". The dirt in your destiny actually adds to the power of your testimony. Sadly, many people leave out the dirt in their destiny, and they want to waive the flowers and fruit of their testimony. However, you can't get flowers, nor fruit without dirt. Joseph has the unpleasant experience of seeing dirty deeds done to him at the hands of his brothers. The pit is dirty literally, then there are the things which are heinously evil that they do after throwing him into the pit. They sell him to some Ishmaelites who are traveling to Egypt.

Egypt in the scriptures always represents a place of bondage and slavery. To sell your brother to some strangers is evil, and downright dirty, but again I have to say that it was his "des-ti-mony". Elevation comes with things that we don't include when we tell people how we got to where we are. It comes with things that make us cry even after we have become successful, and things which make us sad if we think about it too long. There are many untold pieces that are missing from the stories successful people tell. They talk about the stocks and the growth of the business, the sales, the net worth, yet they never tell what they had to sacrifice to get there. We would be shocked how much dirt has gone into the ivory walls of lush mansions and plush penthouses, as well as businesses that we deemed legitimate. Dirt, dirt, and more dirt have been a part of many establishments which are now classified as successful.

Joseph has been sent on an involuntary mission, something which he did not choose for himself, neither would he have ever chosen it for himself. His journey is with a band full of strangers and even though he knew the ones who threw him in the pit, their actions categorized them as strangers also. Being in the hands of strangers and God has a purpose for it? Being thrown in a pit by my own brothers, and there is a purpose for it? Nothing makes sense to you when you have been drafted to go through something that will be a greater benefit to someone else rather than you. It is the very reason that we spend so much time prostrating in prayer asking why me? It doesn't make sense for these people that I know to treat me like they are treating me. Yet it is what is needed in order for me to be positioned and for my purpose to be revealed.

The psychological ramifications can be devastating if you haven't had the confirmation of your vision. Vision will keep you alive in a pit, it will keep you alive through drought and famine. It will also keep you looking for God to deliver you after something happens to you that you don't understand. I have been the recipient of attacks, setbacks, and setups along with every other unpleasantry you can name. However, I have never seen an attack from someone who was always hostile. Most of the time, they were nice and friendly, then they turned hostile after the attack. In Joseph's case, his brothers never liked him. They didn't care for him, nor does the scripture reveal to us that they ever spoke kindly to or about him. I lift that to reveal to you that it is a different kind of attack. He was cordial to them, and when you look at it deeper, his kindness was really never affected by how they treated him.

There is a place of assurance in the heart of the chosen that can't be changed by the outside actions of others. This is why we would again help those who have done us evil, well at least some of us will. If you can't understand the attack, you can't understand getting mad with the attackers. It is something that is totally out of your hand and out of your control. However, what I can control is how I feel and how I handle what has happened to me. At some point, you must talk to yourself regarding the place that you are in. It's a dirty place, and it's a lonely place. Yes, you have been betrayed by people, but your destiny is unfolding, and it will all make more sense after a while. Underestimating the season that you are in will sometimes make you feel more vulnerable. However, trusting that God is using this for the greater good helps you to handle the moment.

CHAPTER 5

"STAYING ALIVE BETWEEN DESTIMONY AND TESTIMONY"-

I have found that there is never an easy way out for those who have somebody else's deliverance in their belly. There are things which are so sensitive in content, when someone speaks of them, we weep because we know Grace delivered us from those places, yet some of the emotions we can't shake. Feelings and emotions are two separate things. One of them is natural, but the other one has been made by love, events, trust, aspirations, hope and not to mention time. Feelings come natural-but emotions are tailored. I would go as far as to say emotions are tailored feelings. Such as, I like her, however, but I love her. I like him, but I love him. Yet I need to say, it is more dangerous to invest emotions than it is to invest feelings. "If you make promises in the presence of feelings--you have now invited emotions into the arena. Now the mindset becomes "you can play with my feelings---- but don't play with my emotions."

We are built to handle certain things with certain mindsets. However, there is a place that you can enter in life where your senses run out of gas, and you start to coast uncontrollably; because you are being controlled by another person. That's what compassion is. It is the passion that causes you to come to another's rescue. It is when your storm compels me to intercede, or sometimes interfere with, what is going on around you or with you. However, it's dangerous to do what I just mentioned. It is dangerous because every individual isn't in trouble who acts like they are, and everyone who has been wounded isn't healed like they pretend to be. Many individuals see everybody as the one person that hurt them. It doesn't matter how kind the person is or how sweet the person may be. They are yet angry with the past and the person from the past, and they will ruin every person who tries to heal or help them.

You know you are in bad shape when you can recognize that you have constant battles, yet you reject those who have come to help you fight. The question needs to be asked; "Why do I have to fight a battle for somebody who is fighting me"? Why do I have to be a deliverer for someone who wouldn't come from across the street to help me? The truth is, we are sometimes reaching for people who keep burning our hands; we are calling people to encourage them and they keep putting us on hold. Why am I fighting for someone who will not fight for themselves? Why am I on my face praying for someone who rejects what I am praying for? Why do I keep loaning money to someone who has no intention of paying me back? Yet when they come to me again, my compassion overrides their debt.

Your favor will always outweigh the actions of those who you have been sent to help. The grace which God places on those he chose carries with it a measure of inner strength. Every deliverer travels the same path. Usually, you are sent to people who eventually will turn on you; some, if not all. Ambassador Christopher Michael Stevens was an Ambassador to Benghazi, Libya. He even helped to build schools for the Libyan people. On September 11, 2012, the very people whom he helped to educate stormed the compound where he was and killed him. If you can't handle the fact that the knife that you perhaps one day will pull out of your back might have the fingerprints on it of someone you have helped, you might need to drop out of the race. Because if you stay in it long enough, you will find that you may have many attacks on your way to the liberating power needed to help others!!

I look at Joseph in a two-fold dynamic because if you would note, his life parallels the life of Jesus in many ways. Joseph's Brothers turned on him because of the **kitu-pishannu** (a ceremonial robe) that he wore-that was a coat of many colors which displayed the father's favor that was upon him. Liken unto Jesus, the robe that he wore was a habergeon, a seamless garment. Like the plot that Joseph's brothers brought against him, Jesus had plots launched against him from one of his own inner-circle. But, unlike Joseph, Jesus knew what was going to happen to him. Yet he pressed forward and he had the power to back up from, or stop what was going to happen to him.

I marvel at the bravery of leaders who in treacherous circumstances press forward even in the midst of imminent death, harm, and danger! I think of first responders, when something horrific happens, everyone else is running away from the danger, but they respond by running into the danger. The question has to arise. What makes someone run to what everybody else is running from? You have to be sold out to purpose and chosen by destiny to run into something with your eyes open, knowing that you are sure to die because of your choice.

Joseph gets a pit as transportation to his destiny, a dirty place; all because he wouldn't shut up, he is put there by the hands of his brothers. He has a destiny; he has a destination but he will not get there without going through the hurtful anguish of sabotage. A pit, but a purpose, a pit but a passion, a pit yet he had a vision, and his vision gave him permission to embark upon it with an outcome on his mind. I don't know who I'm talking to, but you have tried to live clean; but you keep encountering dirty people, dirty places, all because you have a destiny, but it's a dirty destiny.

It's dark there, isn't it Joseph? However, I need to tell you that in *photosynthesis* and *germination*, darkness is just as important as light, and it is a necessity for growth! Being brought up in the country in Ringgold, Louisiana when it became night, you discovered what dark meant. I will say you have not really been in the dark until you have been in the dark without the ability to turn on the light when you want. Some of us are in the dark and we can't turn the light on because God is demanding the darkness, because he is commanding us to grow. If you are yet responding to the things which rob you of your peace, in the same way you used to, you have not grown. Growth demands change. If you are going to grow, you have to embrace your season of darkness, knowing it is beneficial to your growth.

Ecclesiastes 11:5 *KJV As, you know not the way of the spirit nor how the bones do grow in the womb of her that is with a child; even so, thou knowest not the works of God.*

We think of babies being conceived, and if we could ask and they could answer us, the question-and-answer sessions would be interesting. It's dark in there, isn't it? Yes-but I'm growing! It's dark here, but I am on my way toward my destiny!!! Someone may ask how dirty is it going to get? The answer shouts back; you really don't want to know! My advice to you is there are times you have to focus on the vision more than the visible. When dust starts to fly or something comes toward our eyes, the first instinct is to close them. We must learn not to focus as much on people and what they do while we are on our way to victory. If you keep your eyes closed, you will not allow dirt to get into them, and stop you from maximizing your vision!!

I want you to imagine being able to see the intent before the outcome, yet you have to command your human self-preservation skills to take a back seat. The first law of survival is "self-preservation". However, because you have the omnipresence of the Holy Ghost, you have perfect sight in the flesh and spirit. There is no barrier between you, time, and eternity. You can see tomorrow like it's right in your face, you can see the intentions before the outcome. Jesus had this ability yet was sitting and eating bread dipped in wine with the one who will set him up to die. He is sitting close enough to feed the one who will betray him, while Judas the betrayer, is saying

Lord is it I? Jesus knows his intentions, and he knows that he has 30 pieces of silver with Caesar's face on it in his pocket. However, there is something much more sinister than that, the one that upon his revelation of who the Master is, the one Jesus said to him "upon this rock, I will build my church" Peter, he is going to deny him. All of this Jesus knows, he isn't blinded from what they will do, he knows, yet he realizes that it is part of a plan that will lead him to his destiny. Gethsemane means oil press. It means the place of the pressing, but if you note it was dark in the pressing place.

"In the process, you must be willing to experience going through things that will dismantle your original design, that you may end up at your ultimate purpose."

Rodney E. Williams

It was dark in Gethsemane, there were no modern lights such as we have on today. Not only was it dark physically, but there was an uncertainty that loomed in the darkness. We all know that when there is no clear direction for us, we will grope in the darkness looking for that thread that will help us to make sense of it all. However, if you note Jesus' enemies brought him some light!!!! God will bring you into the place of understanding, the purpose and plan for your life. Therefore, what you are hesitant about, God will sometimes send a hand to push you into what you will not walk into willingly.

There is a light coming that will guide you to the place of your purpose, whether it be voluntary or involuntary. Your purpose will be revealed. Judas, the one who would kiss him and betray him, brought him some light. Peter, the one who would deny him, brought him light. The power of darkness will never overshadow the power of light. Light has something that comes with it that totally makes you forget the darkness. If you walk into a dark room and feel for the light switch, once you find the switch and the light comes on, you totally forget the darkness. No one stands in a lighted room talking about how dark it was. When the light comes on you embrace it. It's the same way when God reveals to you the hidden motives and agendas of people, you have to see it for what it is, no matter how deceitful it may be, you have to walk in the light of what he has revealed to you.

We preach and teach how shameful it was for Judas to have been with Jesus all of that time and betray him. We say how sad it was that Peter would deny him in the presence of those who were against Jesus. We say it was just downright dirty! Right behind all of that, we start shouting about Jesus's resurrection three days later. I raise that as a pivotal point because if we are to celebrate the resurrection, we have to investigate the darkness, the deceit, and through whom it came that we may understand that destiny is not always pretty, clean, and pristine. There are times that your destiny and your testimony are combined into one; *"des-ti-mony"* my destiny and my testimony are both combined.

When the suffix *mony* is added to a word, it is added to bring an action to the word. Nowhere will you find "de-sti-mony" in a dictionary or encyclopedia, but you will find it at work in your life. If I could define "de-sti-mony" I would say destiny with some power in it. Matters not how you were thrust into where you are, whether it was your choice or someone else's, it will still yield the fruit of power. The things that people do to us sometimes are done with such evil intentions. Yet, it is what God uses to bring us into the place he desires for us to be. The enemy never thought it would work out in your favor. However, here you are wearing a t-shirt with favor on the front. The dirtier the destiny, the more powerful the de-sti-mony; the more the *hater-mony*-the more *powerful the testimony*. I have a dirty destiny. I've been through things that if I was as cute as some people, I would hide it. But since I've had an ugly, dirty- de-sti-mony God has given me a beautiful restoration testimony.

"Ladies and Gentlemen There Has Been A Change of Plans"

Have you ever attended an event and you had already planned in your mind how it would go by looking at the program? The MC will come out and give us a brief interlude, make us laugh a little if it's a joyous occasion, and reassure us if it is a solemn one. The program begins and things are going smoothly according to plan, and all of a sudden, the MC comes back to the mic and says "ladies and gentlemen there has been a change of plans". In life, the depiction in which I described happens more often than we talk about. We all start with plans, we have our itinerary all laid before us, and then something happens and we end up in a place wondering what has transpired.

In order for us to end up where God wants us to be, he has to sometimes change our plans. Many stories have been altered and changed, not because the person decided to change them; but the story has been changed because somewhere between where the individual started, God stepped in and changed the plans for the person's life. Someone planned to be a business owner and God chose them to be a missionary, another planned to be a surgeon and God chartered their path and called them to a ministry of helps. Many times, the fulfillment is not how much money is in your pocket; it's how much joy that's in your heart. You may fight the tugging in your heart and the late nights lying awake because you can't sleep, yet you will always eventually yield to the plans of God.

In order for God to get the best out of you and me, he has to sometimes place us in situations where we will argue with ourselves and then submit to his will for our lives. The argument is not against God, it is with God's will for your life. Does he have a problem with us arguing with him regarding his will for us; no, he doesn't. Love itself is an argument within itself, it encases the question; why do I feel like I feel about this person? Once that question is asked, then the argument starts. For some it may last a week, for some, it may last 25 years into the marriage, and for some, the entire duration of the relationship. There are some people who are arguing within themselves regarding how they feel, and they are married to the source of the argument. Therefore, I state again that God is not upset with us having a gesticulation with him, in regards to him wanting us to take a path that we didn't choose originally.

Then there is the expectation of what everyone else around you expect of you. Many times, it is the biggest battle that we face. Everyone else around us wants us to go this way, and we

75

sometimes go totally against their expectations. There are millions upon millions of people trapped in prisons without bars. They are imprisoned by the opinions of others, stuck with people whom they went on a blind date with simply because they didn't want to hurt the feelings of their friend who set it up. Now here they are, married to someone else's choice for them, had babies for the choice; and now they feel trapped. I've probably taken this a little farther than you wanted to go. However, imagine that; being in a situation that is burdening you, all at someone else's expense. Never allow someone to make a choice for you if you have to live in the same house with their choice.

Joseph's brothers have given him an unpleasant opportunity dressed in the clothes of hate, treachery, and deceit. They have unveiled their hearts and the hate therein so that they could satisfy their jealous rage. Life is a series of choices, chances, and callings. Where you fall in life will be because of one of the three things I just mentioned. You can make a choice, take a chance, or follow your calling. Whichever you choose will ultimately give you maximum grief or maximum peace. I can tell you that following God will require you sometimes to walk away from the opinion of others and walk with him into your calling. This is a hard thing to do. However, it is the only thing that you can do in order to find the peace that comes from being in God's will. There comes a time that we must stop the argument and yield to the calling that is before us. This we must do unapologetically!

Imagine that you have your life already charted and planned, then your heart gets in the way. You have everything aligned and you have everything right where you want it, then here comes Cupid and shoots you with the arrow of love. The Bible is full of situations like I just mentioned. I use this route because there are many people that feel that after a bad choice, or a choice that ran out of goodness, that their lives are over. Yet, there is still life, hope, and opportunities which lie ahead of them. Everyone is not going to remain in a marriage that ends at the cemetery when one or the other dies. Some people's marriages will end at the courthouse. Though that is a shocking statement, you can't stop living at that point, you have to continue. Though there has been a change of plans yet there has not been a change in the purpose that God has for your life. David, when he discovered that Michal, his wife, was as treacherous as her father Saul, he never turned from his purpose. Sampson was to render a great deliverance for Israel over the Philistines. When his love Delilah revealed the secret to the source of his strength, the Philistines blinded him. However, he still accomplished his purpose when he used his strength to pull down the palace where all the Philistine lords had gathered for a party. Though he died in this attack, he fulfilled his purpose of being.

You Can't Allow A Wounded Heart to Stop Your Gifted Hands....

Rodney E. Williams

The question that may be asked is, "Does changing my mind mean I am double-minded?" I readily answer the question with a categorical no. The reason being is because we change our minds daily in regards to what we will wear, what we will eat, or what movie we will watch. The change that I speak of in this segment is not a general change, but a supernatural one that will affect the lives of others and ultimately fulfill their destiny. There are things that God has spoken to your heart and you think it is just you. However, the tugging on your heart has led you to a place now that you know it is more than just your idealisms floating around in your mind. You realize now that it is God reaching for you that you may reach for others, making you ready for the *announcement; "Ladies and Gentlemen, There Has Been A Change of Plans"* ...

GOD USES LIARS TOO!

One of the most awe-striking things about God is his ability to take a situation that seems to be against you and I, then turn it for our good. I have discovered that in the midst of what seems to be imminent defeat, his hand shows up and reveals to his children his intent. No one has the ability to do that except someone who has the ability to control the good, the bad, and the ugly. I have found that if God gets glory on any level; He will get glory on all levels, from outside of the enemies' plans as well as inside the enemies' camp. Imagine the shock of those who feel they have defeated you, only to find out that they have been defeated themselves. God is the undefeated God; he has a flawless record when it comes to defending his promises and his people. I will say again, the one thing about Satan that we must cue in on is that he is a liar and the father of all lies.

John 8:44 KJV "Ye are of your father the devil, and the lust of your father ye will do. He was a murderer from the beginning, and abode not in the truth because there is no truth in him. When he speaketh a lie, he speaketh of his own; for he is a liar and the father of it.

There are some interesting aspects used in the Bible which open the mind and eyes of the believer to what some call impossibilities. When we take account of how God uses every tool of the enemy against the enemy, it should bring us resurrection hope. The negativists which were used are just as powerful as the positivism's which God used to bring to pass his will for his children. The question has to be asked: why does God use liars and lies, and the answer rings back because the devil will not stop lying! Let's look at this particular instance in the Word of God.

I Kings 22:20-22 KJV

And the Lord said, who shall persuade Ahab, that he may go up and fall at Ramothgilead? And one said on this manner, and another said on that manner.

And there came forth a spirit, and stood before the Lord, and said, I will persuade him.

And the Lord saith unto him, Wherewith? And he said, I will go forth, and I will be a lying spirit in the mouth of all his prophets. And he said, thou shalt persuade him, and prevail also: go forth and do so.

When the hand of God is for you, he will cause you to prevail over your enemy with a rock and a rag, just as he did when David killed Goliath in the valley of Elah. However, when the hand of God is against you, you can have all the military might there is and yet not be able to defeat the army that is in front of you. The strategy God uses is far beyond the comprehension of those who see it for victory or those who suffer from it in defeat. Therefore, the hands of those who have strength, and weaponry to annihilate whom they believe are weak, are bound and rendered helpless because of God's ability.

One of the greatest victories you will ever receive is when God turns your enemies on themselves. The mentioned scripture in I Kings 22 placed the people of God in a situation where they needed their enemies to move in a certain position, but they would not move. The question is asked who shall do it, and the word comes back from God "I shall be a lying spirit in the mouth of their prophets". God has the power inside and outside of your enemy's plans. Never let the enemy bluff you into believing that they have all of the pieces of the dynamic in their control.

We have discovered over and over again that the gloomier the situation, the greater the glory when God shows up. The intention is victory, matters not how he does it, or who he does it through, God will get the victory. Sometimes it's clear cut and you can see it coming, then sometimes it is camouflaged in what looks like utter defeat. There are some of us who are recipients of a last-minute turnaround, in the midst of a situation that looked like it was concrete and settled. I am sure that every child of God has been in a situation or a circumstance that was a closed eye-cliffhanger; but when you opened your eyes, you opened them to a victory that you could only give God the glory for.

The enemy wants us to believe his lies. It is the very reason that he keeps repeating the same thing over and over again to you. It is the methodology he uses in every attack. He strategically places his weapons around us. Once he has placed them around us, he starts to talk. Much like the old westerns we watched, the town gathers a posse and chases the bad guys down. Once they have cornered them in a place, they say to them "we have you surrounded, throw down your weapons, and come out with your hands up". The difference between the posse and the devil is the posse was right, but the devil is wrong. We are never left without a way out. God keeps revealing himself over and over again to us, and he keeps proving to us that Satan is a liar.

There are things that are said sometimes and when they are spoken, they are spoken with the intent to slander or to sabotage others. Yet the destiny of those who have been slandered has been charted by the God who controls all things, even lies. How frustrating it must be to do all you can against someone, and yet they seem to evade everything that you do. Sometimes the things that the enemy sends out as weapons are the things which God uses to magnify his power over the powers of the enemy. The most embarrassing moment to some is when they believe that they have moved from a low level to a higher one, and they encounter someone who knew them from their past. The fear sometimes arises in their throat and they believe they will be defamed because of what an individual might say to defame them or pull them down.

If your past is threatening your present, it is because you are not delivered from it. Anytime you are truly delivered from the past, you never feel threatened that it will show up. Even if someone shows up and brings up your past, there is an adverse reaction to it. If a person is truly delivered from their past and someone brings up something from the past, it reveals just how far the person has come. In essence, it causes the person that the individual tried to defame to measure their progress to know that is who I used to be. Sometimes it actually makes the individual feel brand new all over again.

The projective intent of God is to get you so far ahead of what the devil has said regarding you that it will only exist to the devil and not to you. There is a place in God that he can elevate you unto that what is said regarding you will never reach you. Never let what a noncontributing voice says hinder you from reaching your potential. Hecklers and naysayers have no power over what God is doing, neither do lies and liars, and some of them just like hearing themselves talk!

CHAPTER 6

WHY DO LIES SOUND SO GOOD?

Many times, it is bamboozling the things that are sometimes said about others, which has no supporting evidence to corroborate its validity. It is hard to sometimes fathom the nerves of some individuals to even repeat the things that are sometimes said regarding others. We have been duped by politicians, fooled by advertisements regarding products, that when we opened the box looked nothing like what we saw on the infomercial. Companies spend billions of dollars to present an image that tricks the eye, and when they add the right convincing voice to the ad; there you have it, another lie sold for $59.95!

Lying has become the driving force to gain wealth, influence, and prestige. Yet for some reason or another, even though we have been lied to time and time again, we end up the victim of another scam, another advertisement, and sadly, another person. Which reveals to us that there is something that is within our makeup that makes us believe what is said to us or what is shown to us. When you investigate the just mentioned subject, you would have to ask the question: what could someone say that would make a person believe the next lie when the last 30 promises were all lies.

There are always individuals who rejoice at seeing other people fail. This has become the way up seemingly to some, and the way out to others. Someone has gone through a scandal and finally, they see the light at the end of the tunnel and they try to start a new life. Instead of giving the person a second chance many times, the individual's past is brought up and they end up crushed all over again. Sadly, that story has been played over and over again in the lives of individuals who just want to get back up. They have been down for so long that year after year the lies pile up atop of them when the truth is the infraction was not even that serious. Yet because gossip *sells* and truth *sails,* people continue to add injury to insult. It sounds good; it feels good that someone that you call your enemy has fallen into hard times or a bad stroke of luck. Adding insult to injury is the way that people sometimes feel they are getting the edge on other individuals.

One of the hardest things to deal with is when the face comes off the liar and you find out where it all came from, and how it all began. There is this game that I am sure that many of you have played or participated in. It is when one sentence is told to one person and then it is passed around the room to everyone secretly. The last person then gives the message aloud so that everyone can hear what was said. The clincher is that the message has been totally rearranged by the time it goes around the entire room. That is what happens many times with things that destroy the lives of people or damage their reputations. What was done first is never the last thing which was said. The question needs to be asked: why do lies sound so good and why do people seek to destroy others' lives, even if they have to lie.

The Bible is full of situations that allowed someone to be defamed, shamed, and sometimes even blamed for something that they did not do, yet it was all for the glory of God in the end. The question must arise. If God wants me blessed, why not just bless me without all of the things that I have to go through to receive the blessing. That is one dynamic of looking at it. However, God gets more glory when the enemy creates more havoc, heartache, heartbreak, and then he steps in and totally upsets the devil's plans. Can you imagine how the atmosphere was when Lazarus died in Bethany? *(John 11 KJV)* Let us take a close look at it. Here is a family that loved Jesus, and Jesus loves them even amid this grievous situation. Jesus was their friend. They were his friends. They sent for him to come to them because Lazarus was sick. Surely, he would come; after all, he is Jesus. Yet Jesus didn't come until Lazarus was dead.

This entire situation is the making of a good falling out between friends. Simply because of the inability of one friend in the dynamic, not doing what the other friends wanted him to do. However, when Jesus shows up, he totally transforms the entire situation. He asked where Lazarus was buried, and he stood at his tomb and called him back to life. The next chapter says they were sitting down eating and people were peeking in the window to see what a miracle looks like because Lazarus was just that, a miracle. Beloved it is amazing how God can take something that is horrible in the beginning and make it Holy at the end!

What is the psychology behind someone feeling empowered when someone else has suffered the worst thing that has ever happened in their life? Many people seem to gain power over another person by saying "now we are equal, I was down, and now you are down"! Yet, that is not the intention of God for his children, nor is it the intention of God for his children to feel that way about their enemies. The feeling of empowerment over someone who has fallen into sin, or a scandal, should never be used as an opportunity to degrade or pull another down, but rather to lift them up and place them in a place of restoration, reconciliation and bring one to penitence.

When we view the Bible and we look at its origin and its outcome, we know that God and his providence are at work in its pages. Though God is at work in the pages of the Bible, we also have to realize that sometimes God's works are not as we have been taught. The works of God are sometimes the sin and bad choices of mankind, yet God uses bad choices and sin to bring about his divine ability for a greater good and purpose. How can that be? How is that possible? How can a good God take things which are not good and allow those things to be used as tools to bring about his purpose? The answer to that is quite simple, the human will. One of the strongest things that each of us possess is our will. Your will is so strong that God himself never attempts to take control of any individuals will at any time. The will of every person has been handed to them by God encased in their humanity, yet though God is the giver of our will, he doesn't overtake it nor does he try to do so.

Isaiah 1:19 "If ye be willing and obedient ye shall eat the good of the land"

In order for God to get the glory out of us, he doesn't have to trick us. His desire is not for us to wake up one day serving and praising him, and then ask the question how did I get here. No, God's desire is for us to with our own will, choose him as the Lord of our lives. While we are on our way to choose him and become who he has ordained for us to be, we wear the nature of the first Adam. This is where most of the problems arise in every individual's life. The nature of the first Adam encases the lying tongue, the rebellious heart, and the deceitful ways which caused Adam to be expulsed from the garden of Eden.

James 3:5-8 (KJV)

Even the tongue is a little member, and boasteth great things. Behold how great a matter a little fire kindleth!

And the tongue is a fire, a world of iniquity: so is the tongue among our members that it defilieth the whole body, and setteth on fire the course of nature, and it is set on fire of hell.

For every kind of beasts, and of birds, and of serpents, and of things in the sea, is tamed, and hath been tamed of mankind.

But the tongue can no man tame; it is an unruly evil, full of deadly poison………

The tongue is one of our deadliest members if we don't take account of what it can do to us and those around us. What we say regarding others and ourselves is said with the tongue. One of my greatest lessons came when I learned *"death and life are in the power of the tongue and they who love it shall eat the fruit thereof"*. *(Proverbs 18:21 KJV)* Though I have that revelation and have learned the importance of watching what you speak, so many others have not. Some pride themselves on whose life can I destroy next, who's ministry can I ruin, what individual will believe me without investigating what I say?

They don't care regarding the repercussions which take place, how many homes did this lie destroy, how many hearts are broken. They do not care if they are labeled as being the culprit who started it all. Fifteen minutes of being famous are all they seek. We are at a time where people have become more interested in lies than in the truth. Truth lives in a high place, and in order to remain a person who embraces truth, you have to love truth and understand that truth is a spirit.

John 16:13-14 KJV

Howbeit when he, the Spirit of truth is come he will guide you into truth: for he shall not speak of himself; but whatsoever he shall hear, that shall he speak: and he will shew you things to come.

He shall glorify me: for he shall receive of mine and shall show it unto you.

Those of us who have been chosen as children of God and have received the Holy Ghost we have a mandate to speak the truth, untainted, unbiased, and unrestrained. There is no child of God who loves lies and hates the truth. If you hate the truth and constantly filter lies from your mouth, there is a great chance you have not been redeemed by the blood of the Lamb.

JOSEPH IS GONE, BUT GONE WHERE?

There is no logical reasoning for many of the heinous things which happened to people at the hands of others. No human explanation can ever soothe the trauma that individuals are left with after living through the acts of others toward them. The intention is sometimes more heinous than the result because the results are very much different when God has a plan that will be revealed through the actions of others. So many times, I have been in situations and circumstances that placed me where the enemy didn't intend for me to end up. Joseph left a ditch in Dothan for a fruitful destiny that was financed through the hands of his brother's evil intentions for him.

Can you imagine them going home with the satisfaction of thinking that they had gotten rid of him and shut his mouth from speaking of his dreams? Yet they aren't aware of the fact that they have been used by God in their attempt to misuse him. We serve a God who finances our lives and levels through strange methods, evil actions of frenemies', and setups of others. The question is always asked, can God get us there without going through "Haterville"? The answer comes back yes, he can get us there without bypassing our enemies-yet the journey is more fruitful when we can go through what others have done to us, and yet end up where God wants us. Signed, sealed, and delivered, Joseph went into his destiny with his enemies' fingerprints upon him. I said that because every enemy will turn out to be useful, every attack that they commit will turn out to be profitable to you when you look back in retrospect.

The absenteeism of Joseph satisfied those who hated him, yet it projected him toward the fulfillment of his God-given destiny. The existence of your presence on any soil will manifest your purpose. Which simply means that wherever you land, God is going to manifest your purpose. As a matter of fact, sometimes he can't reveal your purpose until you walk on soil that hasn't been trodden by those who disavow who you are. Many times, others can readily spot your uniqueness and gifting when those around you have reduced your gifting to nothing.

If enough people conglomerate and come against you, it will try you in a way like no other. The only way that you survive group attacks is you have to know that beyond a shadow of a doubt that God is with you. Multiplied outside opinions will either confirm to you that you are made from something supernatural, or disaffirm who you think you are by causing you to turn away from your chosen place.

Yes, Joseph is gone, but the question is: gone where? Don't ever let where your enemies push you, annul where God is using your enemies to take you! There is an adverse reaction, with a definite assurance built within the actions of those who launch evil attacks against you. There is a door revealed when a door is slammed in your face. There is a yes built in the no you keep hearing from those who refuse to see who you truly are. Joseph must've felt totally destroyed from every aspect, yet he kept breathing. The next breath you take must be taken with the mindset of, if I'm breathing, I yet have a purpose beyond the pain I feel. There are some things that are not nice, but they are necessary.

It wasn't nice for all of this to happen to him; however, it was necessary that he could arrive at his destination and be in a position for the transition. There are some people who are born to stand in places of affluence in order that they may build a bridge for others. Key people are key players when it comes to the survival of others. When you look at a person and see that they have lived their lives being everything for everyone else, it simply means that they are key players in the game of life and in the lives of others. What does that mean? It means that there are many pits with that person's name on them. There are many setups and setbacks in the path of that individual, yet they never turn back nor give up. The confirmation that God is with you is revealed in the outcome of the setups, roadblocks, and pits that didn't kill you nor stomp out the fire you have within.

Joseph is gone, but where is he gone? He is gone into a destiny that includes everybody that was in the plan to destroy him, everybody who snarled and laughed at him while they stood around the pit, he was placed in. How noble it is to become a sacrifice for someone who wouldn't even throw you a rope to help pull you from a low place, yet you are going to redeem them from a place of trouble. There are some of you that your feelings and self-esteem have been trampled under the feet of those who have done nothing but taunt you and have taken you for granted time and time again.

Yet, because the fire of destiny burns in your heart, you use each attack as if it was a piece of firewood on a cold winter day.

The enemy keeps piling up evil and you keep throwing it on your fire. It is what kept Joseph alive. It kept him in the pit, it kept him while he was tied and bound on his way to Egypt to be sold by strangers. You can't let it kill you, you have to use it as a motivation to keep you alive through every attack. This is why every time something happens, we must say to ourselves, "I will not fall apart because this is a part of the purpose I was chosen for. I don't know what part it will play in my outcome; however, I know that it is a part of what God is doing in me, through me, and with me."

Joseph didn't know what was happening to him and neither could he process it through his childlike innocence. When your heart is pure and you have no evil intentions for others, you will never understand why someone would do you evil. There is a part of us that accepts what someone does to us if we have in some kind of way invited that into our lives. However, when you have no behaviors in your character that mirror the evil that you receive from someone, it can be traumatizing. Then there is also a peace that provides you understanding where there is none in regards to what happens to you. God is working through what we don't understand, and he is birthing through us a new level of power through what we can't figure out. Finally, he is preparing us to be something for someone else, and that someone might be the one who has placed us in peril, and in Joseph's case, in a pit. If their plot works, it is because the plan is working. *Romans 8:28 KJV "And we know that all things work together for the good, to those who love God and those who are called according to his purpose".*

BUT THE LORD IS WITH ME

Genesis 39:1-4 KJV

And Joseph was brought down to Egypt; and Potiphar, and officer of Pharoah, captain of the guard, and Egyptian, bought him of the hands of the Ishmaelites, which had brought him down thither.*

And the Lord was with Joseph, and he was a prosperous man: and he was in the house of his master, the Egyptian.

And his master saw that the LORD was with him and that the LORD made all that he did to prosper in his hand.

And Joseph found grace in his sight and served him: and he made him overseer of his house, and all that he had he put unto his hand..

One of the greatest feelings you can have is when God's hand is revealed to you when you are in the fight of your life. Even if he doesn't deliver you from it at the time that you think that he should, you are at ease because he has revealed he is with you. The only reason that some people have survived is because of the confirmation of God's presence. The presence of the Lord is the only assurance one needs to live day to day, moment to moment, until full deliverance takes place. The confirmation of God's presence doesn't mean that you will not cry, it does not mean that you will not feel abandoned; it means that you have what is necessary to press forward until God reveals to outsiders what you already know.

Joseph is carried to Egypt by total strangers, placed on an auction block, and sold as a slave. What has happened to him is totally unimaginable, especially knowing that it is done at the hands of his own brothers. Yet, though it seemed heinous from the sight of the natural, it was the unfolding of one of the most awesome presentations of God's providential power. The power God has in his hand is not limited to pretty presentations, it controls the ugliest of circumstances, and it gives birth to testimonies that seem fictitious when they are told. Joseph is sold to a prosperous man, a man who had an influential position with Pharoah, a man who though he was on heathen territory, knew God, and recognized when his hand was upon someone. He looked at the prosperity of everything that Joseph did and realized that when the Ishmaelites brought Joseph down to Egypt, God's favor came with him.

The favor of God doesn't have boundaries, nor does it regard distance, bars, chains, judgements, and the opinions of others. Many times, what you have will be overlooked by those you are around the most, yet readily recognized by others who are strangers. Familiarity has caused many anointed, gifted vessels to spend their entire lives stuck in mediocrity, all while being stepped over and looked over by those around them. People are sometimes called from other places to come to other states and perform. However, when most of the people they send for, if they held something in their hometowns, the attendance would probably drop. The same person can go to another place and pack an arena, simply because they have something that those whom they grew up around can't see. Simply put, familiarity can be blinding.

What Joseph possessed was unique. He didn't have to brag about it, nor announce it. He just served in whatever position he was placed in, and it just flowed through him. Your natural ability to be what God has called you to be will flow from you, even when you are just going about your daily occupation. Not only will others detect it, those who want to normalize you will detect it as well. Many times, people who aren't on your level of gifting will sometimes choose the lesser gift because of intimidation. This I will never be able to understand, for the Bible says "*iron sharpens iron*". *(Proverbs 27:17 KJV)* Which denotes to me that if I am going to be better than what I am, I need to be around someone who provokes me to be better. The word *"educe"* is where we get our word educate. *Educe: means to compel someone to come to a higher level.*

Joseph displayed an ethic that was far beyond anyone around him, and it was noticed! I speak to everyone that is reading this and I say to you that though you feel overlooked, you are noticed. It seems like an oxymoronic statement for me to say that the reason you are overlooked is because you are noticed! Therefore, I admonish you to view being overlooked as God's way of getting you to your place of destiny in a nice-nasty fashion. Joseph's family heard what he said but yet couldn't see what God was doing with him. The words you speak will reveal the heart of the people you speak them to. They will show you how they feel about you by how they respond to you when you speak. The pit was a direct response to how they felt about him. People overlooking who you are to choose the lesser gift is God's way of telling you, yes; but not here! "Yes; but not here", is a hard statement to receive, when you don't have a clue of why you are being rejected in the first place! When God makes that statement to you, you will either groan or grow.

This challenge is the most difficult challenge that you and I will face because it is one that will try our natural and spiritual man at the same time. Joseph is Godly. He has integrity that is second to none. This is dangerous if you are weak. However, weak he was not. Potiphar committed everything he had to Joseph and placed him over all his affairs in his house. He was favored; he carried out the duties daily, ran the house with precision and everything his master owned was in his hands, except his wife. Joseph was approached by his master's wife in an inappropriate way. To place it plainly, she wanted to have sex with him. Satan's main entrance to every woman and man is through fleshly desires. If he gains control of you through your flesh, he can interrupt your future.

God is with Joseph, not only that, but the hurt that he has suffered from his family is with him as well. He is in a very vulnerable moment and he is in a very powerful position. However, he has won the argument of what he will and what he will not do. I want to challenge everyone that is on the porch of elevation and you are about to walk in the doorway of your new level. You must make a covenant with yourself now, in regards to what you will and what you will not do! Temptation is the biggest trap Satan has, and if you are tempted easily, you will never walk into the fulness of what God has for you. If pretty women are your temptation, you are already defeated because Satan will give you as many as you want. If good-looking, robust, muscular men are your flavor, you will always be somewhere stuck in the muck and miry clay of temptation.

Potiphar's wife wasn't going to take no for an answer. Her main objective became I want this new man Joseph-and I am going to have him. Joseph's position and loyalty was to his master Potiphar, and his response to her was "your husband has trusted me with everything he has and has withheld nothing from me except you-and I will not do this evil". The word of God says *"blessed is the man that endureth temptation, for when he is tried, he shall receive a crown of life, which the Lord promised to them that love him".* **(James 1:12 KJV).**

Joseph was determined that he would not fail nor fall prey to this woman, who wanted nothing but to satisfy her lustful, insatiable desires. One day he went into the house to do his business, and while he was doing his business, she grabbed him and said "lie with me" and he snatched away from her and ran out of the house. However, she had a portion of his clothing in her hand. It was his action that revealed that he would never give in to her. Therefore, she decided if I can't have him, I will destroy him. Since he doesn't want me, rather than live in the humiliation that I have tried to force myself upon a man who rejected me, I will make him regret his action. She took the piece of his garment and laid it beside her. When Potiphar, her husband, returned, she told him this conjured-up version of her story, and of course, her story placed all the fault upon Joseph and her husband. She told him you have brought this Hebrew in our house and he tried to rape me, and when I refused, he ran out. Here is his clothing to prove it!

Proverbs 6:34-35 KJV

For jealousy is the rage of a man, therefore he will not spare in the day of vengeance

He will not regard any ransom; neither will he rest content, though thou givest many gifts.

Mrs. Potiphar hit her target-but still she missed her man! Potiphar was enraged against Joseph for what he had tried to do to his wife. However, he didn't realize that his wife was nothing but a lust-filled sleaze who was having her run and filled with all the males in his house and every man that she could seduce. She stirred her husband to rage and jealousy. It was exactly what she intended to do. Again, I say she hit her target, but her scheme could never detour the hand of the God who controls, even lies and liars. She was aiming at Joseph but yet she couldn't get him, because her action did something that she would have no idea of until his true purpose would be revealed. There are many men who have been defamed in this same way by women who couldn't have them yet wanted them. Her attempt to hurt Joseph was her greatest accomplishment because it would be the right action needed to place him exactly where God wanted him to be.

The lie that was told of Joseph was one that placed him in great peril. After all, he could have lost his life at the hands of Potiphar. When people perpetuate lies, they never know what will ignite because of the lie which they tell. I know some are saying, well, that is the intention of the lie in the first place. Joseph didn't have any backing, neither did he need any, because he had God. The mindset in which he must've been in was unimaginable. First, you deal with your brethren's treachery and their lies. Now, this nymphomaniac has accused him of something that he did not do-and to top it off, he ends up in prison for it. Many times, we have seen true-life accounts of men who have been locked away for decades because of lies in rape allegations.

It is difficult enough to live with choices that we have made in life, but to have to live with a lie looming over your head, for something that you did not do, is a heavy burden to bear. I mean, you are the new boy; you are the one that Potiphar has made a lord in the house. All eyes are on you and then this woman does this. How much worse can it get? There is a path that you would never have traveled down if you knew some of the things that were going to happen. However, the path was designed to take you to and through some things-that, you might end up on a path you wouldn't have chosen for yourself. I challenge you to not chase destiny because it has so many crooks and turns, pits, poisonous personalities, and dark tunnels that you will never be able to catch it, anyway. Your destiny is going to be revealed to you through some things that you would not call purpose, power, nor would you call it pretty. Yet it will reveal to you the will of God **for** your life.

IT WORKS BETTER IN THE DARK

There is not a more welcoming sight than when you have been without power for whatever reason, and all of a sudden, the lights come on. It is the same way when you have been gifted to shine the light of hope into the lives of others. The one who shines light into the lives of others -have sometimes gained the ability to help others from being in dark places themselves. Nothing is more powerful than an eye-witness! This is why when we view our court system, an eye-witness account is the most valuable testimony in the courtroom. It is through their account that the case can be opened and shut. Just as an eyewitness is valuable, so is someone who has survived the challenges of life. When a witness tells their story, there is a certain solidity and assurance that is in the air that you know you are in the presence of truth. It matters not to them the pain that they have suffered, the adrenaline that they thrive from is that they have the truth-the whole truth-and nothing but the truth.

Many times, others live through what is designed to kill them because they have been lied on by someone who had the intention to destroy them. Every day they arise with vindication on their mind, that one day they will live to see time tell their story. When you have a people's purpose, your main goal is to see someone else come through what has tried to kill them. In Joseph's case, he is in a position that he has been thrust into prison under the looming suspicion of guilt. However, he is innocent. Being innocent doesn't remove the feeling that comes along with being falsely accused. The hurt is still present, the shame is still there, the guilt of being around the individuals whom sometimes you knew had an ill will, yet you still tried to befriend them. The only thing that keeps you alive when you are innocent is that you know God is righteous and he will reveal himself in your situation sooner or later.

Joseph is in a dungeon, it is a dark place, gloomy no doubt, smelly, and everything else that comes along with such a place. However, the Bible says, *"But the Lord was with Joseph and gave him favor with the keeper of the prison". (Genesis 39:21 KJV)* The fact that the Lord is with you is the one thing that gives you the edge over every demon and dilemma you are facing. The fact that God was with him placed him in an influential position, though he was locked in prison. Many times, our voices are magnified when others need us rather than just notice us. There are people that are noticed and, for some reason, yet they aren't recognized. The anointing will move you from being noticed to being recognized. Joseph had a natural anointing, which means that he didn't have to have music. He didn't have to sing a song or any of the things we use in this modern era to set the atmosphere. He was naturally anointed.

There are some people who have *natural anointing*. Because they have it, they have the ability to enter a room and speak from the heart of God, things that others will have to fast for days and sometimes weeks before they enter into that realm. Pharaoh has placed two individuals in prison. They are there during the time when Joseph is there, a baker and a butler. Construction workers build bridges out of concrete and steel, but God builds bridges from people. He uses the connections we have with others, whether purposely or accidentally, to connect us to the place he wants to take us. Not only that he will use what they are dealing with to sharpen the gifts that he has given unto us. The trials of your acquaintances are their cries for help.

Joseph was in prison, but he was also in a position! Being in a position can come in many different forms. However, it can be one of the most uncomfortable places for you. Not only can it be uncomfortable, but it can also be unnoticeable to the person that is in a position for their greater. There are times I have stood before people to prophesy to them, and I have told them where you are is right where God wants you to be. That is not what you want to hear, especially when it is the worst place that you have ever been in your life. The absenteeism of turbulency is an indication that you are not soaring nor are you flying. The presence of the abnormalities that we face are indications that we are in the realm of the spirit or we are in demonic territory.

Joseph was both in the will of God and in demonic territory at the same time. I know that one may ask the question, how is that possible, and the answer comes back that most of us are there right now. We are in demonic territory, yet we are in God's will and it is all going on simultaneously. Jesus was in God's will when he was being mocked and accused of being an insurrectionist, but he was in the devil's territory while this took place. If you are chosen by God, the presence of one without the other doesn't exist. Joseph is in prison, but what he doesn't know is that God has controlled every action of every person who has brought him to this point. Again,

I will utter that God can bring you into what he has promised you without trials. However, you will not be able to stay there because of the lack of strength. Some strength you only gain when you go through trials. It's the reason that some people can handle some of the most horrific things that would have killed others immediately.

The stage has been set for Joseph, but it is not a stage with lights and a crowd of on-lookers who are cheering him on. His stage is this dark, horrible place. His crowd are those who are in prison with him, but the producer of the production is God. I aforementioned that Pharaoh was upset with two of his servants, the baker, and the butler. He threw them into prison for whatever crime they had committed. They both had dreams. One dreamed one night, and the other dreamed his dream on a different night. Their dreams were prophetic in nature and they sought the interpretation of their dreams. To be an interpreter of dreams requires you to be connected to God, who knows all and sees all. Joseph was on heathen territory however, the God who sees all and is in every place was with him.

The butler dreamed he saw three vines and in the three vines were grapes and he was passing Pharoah his cup as he had before. While the baker dreamed that he had three white baskets upon his head, the baskets were full of things he had baked. The butler came to Joseph and Joseph said to him this is the interpretation of your dream. In three days, you shall be restored to your position in the palace, and when it is well with thee, remember me, and bring me out of this place. The baker, when he saw the butler's interpretation was good, he asked for the interpretation of his dream and Joseph said the three baskets represent three days. In three days shall Pharoah lift thy head from off thy shoulders. Three days later, Pharaoh had a party and the things which Joseph said came to pass just as he had said. Even in the darkness of the prison, his gift could not be stamped out. Even though the butler received the favorable interpretation of his dream-yet, he forgot Joseph and remembered him not.

I want to encourage someone who has been everything for everybody, all while going through your own challenges and trials. Though the butler forgot Joseph, God did not, though others have forgotten you, God will not forget. The interpretation of Joseph's dream was more than just an interpretation. It was God's way of getting a witness into Pharaoh's palace to give witness to the gift that Joseph possessed. Every act of kindness that you perform on the behalf of others, the things you did without price or expectation of gratification, God is not going to forget. The pain, the hurt, the ridicule of others, and what they do to you does not stop you from operating in your purpose. As a matter of fact, it is those things that make your gift work just that much better. We all have been in dark places, places that we were seemingly out of place, but from that place, we connected to our destiny. Though it seems that God must not know where I am, he knows, though it seems that God must not see what I am going through, yes, he sees.

What I said does not mean that God is insensitive to you and me, and what we are going through. God is more concerned about our purpose than our feelings. My purpose is the reason for my existence. My feelings belong to my body, but my purpose belongs to God. This beloved is a matter between God and your purpose, not between your body and your feelings. If you move by your feelings, you will totally sit idly by and miss the reason that God placed you where you are. The most difficult thing is to do it when it hurts. Sometimes we have to give others a word for their circumstances, but the question has to arise when is someone going to give me a word for mine? I am passing out directions to others to point them toward their next level; but when is God going to send someone to pass me directions for mine? Though we ask all these questions to ourselves, our gift is yet blessing others and giving them what is necessary that they may connect to their purpose. All of this is happening while sometimes we are in a dark place.

Joseph's interpretation of the dream was not the liberation of the butler from the prison, Pharoah's decision was the reason the butler was freed and restored. However, the word of his restoration came from the ability that Joseph was able to interpret what he had dreamed. God navigates our deliverance in strange ways, yet it is because of what he placed on the inside of us that others find their way. This divine encounter with Joseph and the butler was one that God had carefully and methodically put together. It all happened from a place of darkness, a place where there was no physical light. However, the illuminating light of God's revelation shone brightly.

Perhaps you are in a dark place and you have been placed in a situation which totally locks you out, while others are enjoying or even sometimes prospering from your gift. Sometimes you are in a dark place and no one knows it but you, simply because the darkness that I speak of is not literal darkness, the darkness I speak of is when you are in the lonely place of rejection and ostracism. There is no worse place to be than to be lonely and you have a crowd around you. No one feels your pain, no one feels your hurt, nor do they see your struggle. However, everyone is coming to you for answers when you too need answers for the conundrum that you are in. Yet, the oil of revelation keeps pouring from you and the anointing for direction keeps flowing through you. It's because your gift works better in the dark. You have the light for others, and somewhere someone has a light for you.

CHAPTER 7

WHEN IT IS YOUR TIME, NO ONE WILL BE ABLE TO STOP YOU!!!

Many doors have been closed in the face of others because they simply had the wrong last name. However, there is a place in God where the last name, nor individuals who may not want you there, can stop you from being there. Nothing is more disappointing than to hear that a door was shut because someone said something about you that changed the individual's mind about choosing you. Some people's motive is to do all they can to stop others from getting to their next dimension. Even though that happens a lot in the world in which we live, heaven is unhindered by the evilness that's upon the earth. This is why one must know their kingdom rights and authority. My kingdom rights and authority cancel every attack against my name, every evil assignment against my progress, and every mouth that is opened against me in any negative way.

Sometimes the difficulty that comes our way is mainly the reason many people quit or stay in the same situation that they are in. There is a law that comes with success, and that law is perseverance. There is no one who ever became successful by quitting. Difficulties will arise, but you should never allow difficulty to erase the vision that you have burning in your heart, nor should you allow it to quench the fire in your soul. There are certain things that the enemy brings against every individual who has decided to rise and be what God has called them to be. If you have a conversation with successful individuals, it will seem like they are reading from a script, because you will hear the same things repeated. It is because there are some things that come along with the territory.

One of the most difficult things to do is to know that God has chosen you for something special, yet you seem to be so far from the place he chose you to be. The quest and the questions that are before you seem to be so insurmountable to you because of all the things that lie before you. It is the very reason that many people are standing in the midst of success today. All because they had the nerve to go see! We all have to go the distance of our desire. If you do not go the distance of your desire, you will live in the regret of your "what if's". You will never know what God has planned for you if you do not go the distance of your desire. It is within the fire that burns within you that you will find the connection to your purpose. It's the very reason that you exist in the first place. There are some things that only you can contribute. It matters not how insignificant they are to others. It is important that your part is added.

Some may have a major role; however, the supporting cast is just as important as those who have a major role. Without the supporting cast, the movie cannot be fully understood. This is why my heart aches for those who threw away their parts, because they felt they didn't have a major role in ministry, in a family decision, or in life. Your role is major regardless of how minor someone may try and make you seem. Sometimes it takes divorce, death, or someone just quitting for some to see how major someone is in their life. You must never allow how someone else sees you to be the fuel that pushes you. If you ever allow another's opinion to be the determining factor by which you accelerate or descend, you will become like a battery-operated toy. The opinions of others will become the batteries which cause you to run or cause you to be immobilized.

Joseph's moment of destiny was seemingly put on hold-by the fact that the butler forgot him in prison even after he had given him the interpretation of his dream. However, what he didn't know was what he had spoken to the butler was the final piece of a divine plan. He didn't know that God, through a pit, a nymphomaniac liar, a prison sentence, and an ungrateful butler, was about to unveil one of his most powerful examples of divine providence. When it is your time, everything that was supposed to be against you will turn for your good. Your storm is about to turn into your story. It is in this place that Joseph has learned the ways of Egypt. He has learned how to maintain focus despite the fight that he is in, though he doesn't understand it all, it is the place of his confirmation.

There is a place where God confirms all of us, even when it seems that God must not know what is going on with us. The place of our confirmation has everything to do with the area of our purpose and our gifting. For some, it is worse than others because if my gift is to deliver people who are in demonic territory, God will not train me for it in a place where everything is nice and pretty. Your training ground will match your area of gifting. If you look around at those who have great deliverance ministries, you will find that they gained their strength to fight, from places that you would never think they had ever been in personally. What you are anointed to do, you make it look easy because you understand the stages of the fight that you are dealing with. Joseph is about to get the assurance that he is not crazy, nor weird, nor is he fanatical. I say that because everyone who has real faith, at some time or another, is called crazy, weird, fanatical, and might I add a few other things along with it. Simply because what you say doesn't match what others around you see. Yet, you have to remember everybody who can see-cannot see! When I say that, I mean that there are people who have perfect sight in the natural realm but they are totally blind when it comes to spiritual things.

Joseph conceals from everyone in Egypt what he had seen in his homeland prior to being brought to Egypt as a slave. If you notice, he has prospered in every area he has been placed in, but that is not the primary reason that he is in Egypt. His primary reason for being in Egypt is that he might be in place. This is why I have learned to be content with what I go through in my life, because sometimes God is putting us in place for the next season. There may be someone now that's reading this, and you can't for the life of you figure out why in the world you are dealing with some horrible situation, and you don't have any clue why you are in it; it may be that God has put you in place. The only time you will be able to figure out why you are there will be after you have come out of it, and you see the manifestation of the fruit from it.

Pharaoh has some troubling dreams. They are so troubling that he sends for soothsayers, magicians, and astrologers to interpret the dreams. There are dreams that we have and they are just passing memories, which may result from something that we did that day or something that we watched on television before we went to bed. Then there are dreams that we have that we know they are meaningful and they have great significance. Through these dreams, God is trying to tell us something or warn us of something through what we have seen. Then there are times God allows influential people to dream. When I say influential, I speak of someone who has a position from which the trajectory of their position and opinion will influence a nation or a large group of people. When someone influential starts to dream something that is troublesome, usually it is for the greater good of a large group of people. Pharaoh's dreams were unique, and they were chillingly troublesome.

Genesis 41:1-8 KJV

*And it came to pass at the end of two full years, that Pharaoh dreamed; and behold, he stood by the river. ***

And behold, there came up out of the river seven well-favored kine and fat-fleshed; and they fed in a meadow.

And, behold, seven other kine came up after them out of the river, ill-favored and lean-fleshed and stood by the other kine upon the brink of the river.

And the ill-favored and lean fleshed-kine did eat up the seven well-favored and fat kine, so Pharaoh awoke.

And he slept and dreamed the second time; and, behold seven ears of corn came up upon one stalk, rank and good.

And, behold, seven thin ears blasted with the east wind sprunt up after them.

And the seven thin ears devoured the seven rank and full ears. And Pharaoh awoke, and behold it was a dream.

And it came to pass in the morning that his spirit was troubled; and he sent and called for all the magicians of Egypt, and all the wise men thereof; and Pharaoh told them his dream; but there was none that could interpret them unto Pharaoh.

The hard spots for others are getting ready to turn into the spotlight for God to use you for the very reason that you were born. There are some difficult places and difficult spaces that only someone who is purposed will be able to fit in. This is the moment when everything around you and everything that you have been through will begin to make sense. The mere fact that Joseph was in prison for something that he had not done, yet where he was placed, would be the platform from which God would reveal his purpose; is totally mind-blowing. The worst place he had ever been in his life was the holding place for him until his time would be revealed. It is safe to say that though it's the worst place now when God finishes, it will be the best place later on......

Romans 8:28 KJV *And, we know that all things work together for good to them that love God, to them who are the called according to his purpose...*

"YOUR NAME WILL BE CALLED BY SOMEONE WHO THOUGHT THEY FORGOT YOU"

There are moments in life that we ask ourselves where is the fulfilment of my prophecy, where is the unveiling of the masterpiece which I have expected to unfold my entire life. When will I ever arrive at the destination that I have so looked for all my life? I have asked myself many questions in private that I would never have asked aloud in public places. Because of the pain that arises when you ask yourself certain questions, tears follow, and sometimes if we tell the truth, a pity party may follow the tears. There is no story that has been told in totality. There is no story that has been told, and every inch of the person's life was revealed. The reason being is that there are some things that we can't stand to re-live, so we remember them through soliloquizing them to ourselves. When we do this, we also have to learn how to not silently beat ourselves up with something that God has already let us live through.

Joseph has poured out his favor in two different places while he has been in Egypt and both places have seemingly landed him nowhere. He has given Potiphar's house favor and stability, yet his wife lies on him and he lands in prison. He has come to prison and passed out revelations of restoration for the butler and all he asked the butler to do was remember him. Yet, he is still three years stuck in this dungeon. In the midst of our human limited understanding of

God's will and way-we sometimes enter into functional depression. Which means that we are depressed but we are still able to function in the midst of it. The reason we end up in such a place is because the flesh is marking time and times. Time is an enemy to our faith. The reason I say that is because our flesh is on a time limit-yet our faith is not. Faith will be just that, faith. Not old faith, yesterday faith, last year faith, no faith will always be faith, and it is unhindered by time. If you notice **Hebrews 11:1, KJV** opens with *"Now Faith is"*. Which denotes to us that faith is what it was and it will always be what it is; FAITH!

Life will not only cause you to have birthdays and new days, but life will reveal to you days that are filled with unexpected elevation. God is the God of **"Suddenly"**. Joseph was sitting in the prison house, not realizing that something was happening outside of the prison that was beyond the understanding of everyone. Pharoah couldn't understand it, his magicians and soothsayers could not figure it out-yet it was the perfect moment for God to reveal that he is the God of suddenly. We should never become disturbed when it seems that people who we blessed have forgotten our names or our kindness. God is able to make everyone remember your name, even those who intend to forget it. He is also able to make everyone be reminded of every act and action that he used you to help bring others out of their dilemmas.

Hebrews 6:10 KJV *"God is not unrighteous, so as to forget your work and the labor of love which you showed toward his name, in that ye have ministered to the saints, and do minister."*

Joseph's deliverance from prison would not come from a person but it would come from possession, the possession would be from what God had placed on the inside of him. God has placed the power of deliverance inside of us all. You are not mentioned sometimes until what you have is needed by others who act as if they have forgotten you. What we possess places insurance on our coming season. My gift is a key that will unlock a door that no one else's key will fit. God sometimes will cause those who have been overlooked to be recognized through the gift that he has placed within them. There have been many rooms I have sat in that I wouldn't have been there if it wasn't for the gift that God gave me. This tells me that all invitations are not from cordiality. Some are given to you because what you have is a necessity! My word to you is don't worry if what's on the outside doesn't cause you to become noticed, because what's on the inside will. Misused, lied on, falsely accused, imprisoned, forgotten, abandoned, and then ***suddenly!***

The last emotion that you will have to overcome before your breakthrough is the emotion that comes with being abandoned. Abandonment is hard to deal with because it makes you feel that you aren't good enough, or something is wrong with you in some kind of way. Joseph had suffered two different forms of abandonment, one from his own brothers, the other one was from the butler who forgot him and what he had done for him in interpreting his dreams. You may have gone through some of the most horrific things in life, yet you can attest that abandonment is a difficult emotion to overcome. God has always provided for his children a way of escape, regardless of whatever was trying to hold them or prevent them from arriving at their appointed destination. Joseph is about to become ***the recipient of restoration.*** It is at this point that it will be revealed to him the power of being overlooked, the beauty of being abandoned, and the strength of being sabotaged.

I know that each of the words overlooked, abandoned, and sabotaged are words that are not associated with beauty, power, or any other term that prepares one for a favorable outcome. The truth is, when God is controlling each action that happens, it brings whoever is experiencing the action into something favorable. We can't see it because we stand in the face of our adversities and challenges. However, we have to realize that God is coaching our chaos, and he is also trying our adversities. Whoever thought that Job would come through what he was going through, but in the end, he says to God, *"now I know that thou can do all things". **(Job 42:2 KJV)*** It's the end that makes the beginning understandable, no I don't know what this shall turn out to be. However, I know that it shall turn for my good.

Joseph is in prison, yet there is a conundrum going on in the palace that only he has the answer to. God will bring you into your time, or he will bring your time to you. Either way, your time will come. Those who prosper from your gift, and act as if they have forgotten that you ever helped them or imparted into them, is your invitation to the palace. Social and Spiritual Plagiarizers are plentiful in this era. Those who have made their arrival on someone else's gift or shoulders, yet they act as if they got there on their own, will eventually acknowledge they have a bottle, but Joseph has the oil.

It might not be tomorrow, and it might not be next week, but God always arranges circumstances to prove who has the connection that will keep everybody else alive. The person who has the connection with God in a region is usually the one that is ridiculed the most, talked about the most, and placed in unlikely places. In this case, it was Joseph. In your case, it might be you.

Pharaoh's troublesome dreams proved that though he was surrounded by soothsayers, boneshakers, and stargazers, none of them had the power to reveal to him what God was saying to him. God's language must be interpreted by someone who knows God, who walks with him, and who is open to hearing his voice. The magicians, the soothsayers, and stargazers could not tap into what God was saying to Pharaoh. They practiced magic but they couldn't understand the mystical. Though they could not understand the interpretation of the vision that Pharaoh had, they understood that there was a language beyond their power. The butler, though he had no power to interpret dreams, nor was he a magician, God had created a moment for him that he would never forget.

Your connection to your place of purpose will not come from what you did in a high place, it will come from what you did in a low place. This is why you must always allow God to use you just as much in the dark as he does in the light. The butler that Joseph had given a word to was the seed that God would use to bring to light Joseph's purpose for being in Egypt. A seed is planted in a dark place but it brings what happened in the dirt to the light. The butler was the seed that would bring Joseph's ability to the light and to the palace. When everybody had tried their hand at interpreting the dreams of Pharaoh, the butler said "I do remember my faults this day". I decree to you that God is getting ready to bring you up in someone's mind and your name out of someone's mouth; who thought they'd forgotten you.

I prophesy to someone who is reading this that this is your last day in the dark! Joseph didn't know it, but this was his last day in this dark place! While sitting, no doubt doing what he would normally do, he heard his name called "Joseph Pharaoh wants to see you". The emotions that come from deliverance bring back the memories of everything you have been through from the bondage you were in. Joseph left the prison that day, not realizing that he would never return to it. The lies that were told on him by Potiphar's wife had a purpose, even though it had caused him so much pain. The end of your worst is the best of your beginning. This is the place that every attack that you have suffered is rewarded by the confirmation that now you know that God chose you. That's all most of us want who have gone through horrendous trials and tests. We just want the confirmation that we will not die in the dark, but our lives will be a testament that God said to us what we have spoken to others.

Never let what you see override what you know, and never let your emotions get in front of your anointing. There is a pain that will come along with the place that God is taking you to, and if you don't know how to handle the pain, you will never arrive at the place. I have come to a point in my life that I realize that pain is the foundation for gain. If there isn't any pain in the process, then what you are doing is either illegal or you are not operating in the place of your purpose. Purpose has with it, its own special pain; however, you realize that pain is necessary for God to bring to pass what he is doing.

THANK GOD MY UGLY SEASON WASN'T MY ONLY SEASON!

The most beautiful things in life are overlooked because the eyes of those who saw it were stuck on what it was and not on what it could become. Many of us have been left for dead, looked over, and stepped over, all because someone saw our previous season as our only season. I have rejoiced for many things, but one thing I rejoice for is that my ugly season is not my only season. It is the season that God will prove to you who has eyes to see beyond where you are present. Many times, we are trying to show things to people who will never see it, because they can't see beyond the place, they wanted you to remain in. You will never be anything different to some people until what they deemed to be your last season turns into your lasting season. Even after your season changes and you move from there, they will still remember only the part that they want to hold you hostage too.

What you are becoming encases what you were, but in a very different manner. The paper you write on is still a tree, just in a different form. The pencil you write on the paper with is still the tree, just in a different fashion. The desk you are writing atop is a tree. However, it is just in another frame or portrait. So, the paper you write on, the pencil you write with, on top of the desk you write on while sitting in the chair you sit in are all manifestations of the tree. Just as the just mentioned analogy reveals that one thing encases many different things, so does seasons. One season can do so much for you all at one time, yet without you noticing the value of the season. Winter is an ugly season if you are a person that loves green lush grass, butterflies, and plants. Yet there are some plants and flowers that only grow in winter, there is even certain grasses that are called winter grass. So, there are no ugly seasons on God's calendar "he makes all things beautiful in its own time". **(Ecclesiastes 3:11 KJV)**

Every attack that we suffer, every setup and setback, even every lie, has its purpose. I know that doesn't sound good, nor does it feel good. However, it is the plan of God to get us to our place of destiny by any means necessary. It's not our call to choose how we will make our arrival and by what mechanism we will get there. The only thing that we can do is wait for our ride to show up. Those of us who have our own car might remember the time when we didn't, and we had to wait for someone to come and give us a ride here or there. Then we bought our own car, now we can go and come at our own liberty. When it comes to God and his purpose for you, you have to wait for God to send your ride. Unlike waiting for a ride in an automobile, God sends strange things to carry us to our destinations.

Sometimes the ride is pain, heartache, betrayal, and loneliness, yet, when the ride is over, you arrive at the exact place where God wants you to be. There is nothing that we can do in some cases but wait, and while we wait, we focus on what God said to us. Waiting makes us eager, it also makes it easier for us to identify the voice of God. This is why, when we come to the time of vindication, we don't fall to pieces in depression. Waiting produces answers and it also produces the necessary elements that you and I need to fight in the future. When God vindicates you, he does not vacate from our beings the struggle we have had, for it encases the strength that we will need for our next fight and our next level.

Joseph has been through an ugly season! He has gone through something that cannot be washed off or washed away. There are things that we go through that we cannot detach ourselves from, it is a part of our makeup and our spiritual, as well as our social DNA. If we moved across the world to another continent, it would still be a part of us, it would still arise from time to time. However, though it is a part of us, it's that part that makes us embrace the pretty parts of our lives. All of us have some places in our lives that are ugly to us, yet they complement the beautiful places which God has given us. Divorced, pregnant out of wedlock, stuck in a midlife crisis regarding a bad choice you've made, that you spent years trying to make into something that it would never become. Yet, in the midst of all that, God shows up and speaks to you and says, I want you to keep all of the ugly things you have, but take this joy, peace, and strength to add to what you already have.

Your life is not over at the expense of another's choice. God didn't design life to be that way. Joseph's brothers put him in the pit, sold him out of their presence and possession. Yet their choice was about to be overridden by God's favor that was upon his life.

121

I decree that God's favor will override every attack and attacker that has tried to come to thwart or throw you off your course. This is the one thing that the devil didn't plan for. He arranged all of his weapons, situated all of his witches and warlocks, but he didn't factor in God overriding his attacks. If the enemy won a fight, he only won because God will use that win to turn it into your victory. One fight does not equate the whole battle. Faith breeds hope and hope gives us the assurance that wherever we are that help is on the way. Joseph's request to the butler, "And bring me out of this place for I have done nothing to be here" is the first time that we hear of him seeking to understand why he was in his trial. It's an ugly season for him. Like Joseph, many times, we comb our hearts and ask the question "why am I here"? I have given my strength to help people get to places that I myself have never gone to, and they get there and try to kill me socially. "Why am I here"? I have picked up others to give them another chance, only to find out that the reason they were dropped was because they deserved to be, but I couldn't see that. There are a lot of emotions that come up when you are in an "ugly season".

Then, just when you thought that you were in a place where it would all end for you, God reveals that everything that you have suffered has all been planned to bring you to a certain place for a specific time. There are many individuals who found the best moment in their worst experiences. Their strength was revealed in how much they went through while they were under pressure. There is nothing that can empty the pain from your life that you have gone through, but there is a joy that comes to you, *"that after you* *have suffered a while, the Lord shall make you perfect, establish, strengthen, settle you." **I Peter 5:10 KJV*** The "Ugly Season" is getting ready to unfold into the most beautiful thing that one never suspected. Joseph has had to do the unthinkable-yet the unthinkable has proved that he is unbreakable. To stay alive in what you don't understand is one of the most difficult things to do. Yet, you did it! God has a reward for those who trust him when they don't even understand what he is doing. After all that time in Egypt, being lied on, unjustly imprisoned, abandoned, and forgotten, but one day his name was called. The statement that followed was "Pharaoh wants to see you in the palace".

Can you imagine how many thoughts must have riddled Joseph's mind? Why? What have I done? Is he going to kill me like he killed the baker? When you have been mistreated for a long length of time by people, it will cause you to sometimes feel that things will not get any better for you. The expectation of bad news after bad experiences has become normal for some people. Yet there is an elite group of individuals who have faith in God that "it won't always be like this". God has a set time for those of us who have been through the darkness for someone else's deliverance. There are people who have suffered the worst situations and circumstances, all because they had been chosen to be the deliverer for someone else. I know that some will say that it is unfair for someone to have to bear someone else's burden. When it comes to saving someone's life to preserve the purpose of their life, God will go through great lengths. It is important to understand that the next generation that's coming on must have a bridge from the past to their future. Your name is being called Joseph. Pharaoh needs you to come to the palace. After this long ugly season, after this dark night, this treacherous trek; God is about to reveal that "Your Ugly Season Is Not Your Only Season..."

YOU CAN TAKE YOUR TIME BECAUSE NOW ITS YOUR TURN

Psalms 31:15 KJV My times are in thy hand; deliver me from the hand of mine enemies, and from them that persecute me.

Vindication is a sweet victory when you have all of those standing around you who have accused you falsely. They have said all manners of evil against you predicated upon someone else's outside opinions. They spoke evil against you, and you were in no position to prove your innocence. Then vindication comes and everyone is all apologetic to you because they now know the truth. But how do you feel when there is no crowd around you, yet down on the inside you know that you are not guilty of anything that you have been accused of. Sometimes, the anointing that you possess is the confirmation of your innocence. Many times, people will falsely accuse you and never come back to apologize nor repent from what they said or done. *Psalm 37:6 KJV "He will vindicate you in broad daylight, and publicly defend your just cause."*

Joseph's anointing is the confirmation of his innocence. God has a way of speaking the truth from the anointing that he places on the accused in the midst of the accusations they face. Joseph's life has been a series of accusations, one after the next. His brothers accused him of being a dreamer who sought the opportunity to exalt himself above them. Not only that, his father rebuked him as well for seemingly insinuating that he was exalting himself above him and his mother. One accusation after another, from which he had no vindication; the only vindication that he had was his visible anointing. The anointing is both judge and jury to the onlookers who have judged God's chosen falsely. Joseph was absent of a crowd of supporters, yet he had a crowd that was plenteous when it came to accusers.

There will be a time in everyone's life that only God will be able to reveal to others your true identity. There are many individuals who have spent their entire lives trying to fight for themselves, only to end up with mounds of legal fees and articles regarding their fight. Truth is pregnant, and it has to give birth sooner or later. What sends the truth to the labor room is the righteousness of the God we serve, who will put to rest every lie and liar when it comes to the vindication of his children. Joseph is God's secret weapon that he will use to save many other individuals' lives. Does Joseph know that? No, he doesn't know it. All he knows is that his name has been called by Pharaoh to come to the Palace. Have you ever been hurt to the point that it stifled your expectation that you unconsciously started to settle for your present because it seemed that your promise wasn't coming? Acclimating to what you aren't supposed to be around will sometimes take hold of you and semi consciously stifle your expectations.

Then there is the reaction of confidence. The reaction of

confidence is when you know that you know you have not done anything that merits what you are receiving from those around you. Confidence will place a rigidity in your demeanor that some will mistake as meanness. There is a place in your trial that the only thing that will keep you sane is confidence. Joseph is kept alive and sane in Egypt simply because he has a level of confidence that was far above the level of treachery which he had suffered. It's the only way to stay alive in a foreign place. It's the only way to stay alive in the midst of a battle that you can't understand why you are in it in the first place.

Joseph wasn't in a hurry to get to the Palace after coming out of prison. His demeanor, according to the scriptures, says he had respect for Pharaoh. He wanted to take a bath and change clothes, of course. However, there is a subliminal demeanor that is spoken in his behavior. A demeanor that speaks to his self-respect and his dignity. That demeanor is "I'm not in a hurry to hear the news of whatever is going to be said, I'm sure whatever it is, can't be any worse than what I have suffered." I want you to note that Joseph's behavior is totally different from the behavior of those who came to get him from prison.

Genesis 41:14 KJV *"Then Pharoah sent and called Joseph, and they brought him hastily out of the dungeon, and he shaved himself, and changed his raiment and came in unto Pharaoh".*

The anointing that is in your life is not hindered by time, space, power, people, or principalities. Witches, warlocks, soothsayers, and boneshakers have no power that parallels the power of God. So that means that the power of God is the only power in the earth realm! Joseph is called upon by Pharoah and he simply takes his time. He doesn't rush into the chamber where Pharaoh is, but he takes a shave, bathes, and changes his clothes, and then he comes into the palace. It's his turn now, it's his moment, and it is the opportunity for God to reveal his power in heathen territory. It is God's opportune moment to reveal Joseph's purpose in the midst of his persecutors. I speak from a level of experience that sometimes you have been so bombarded by the accusations and attacks of those who want to destroy you that only God can vindicate you. If you notice, he is not trying to tell his side of the story. He never sits down and says to anyone, "see this is how it went". There is a place in the heart of the chosen that is sanctified only to the purpose of God and it awaits the fulfilment of the truth. That tells me to tell you it's dangerous to attack someone who doesn't counterattack you. The old antic "if I hold my peace and let the Lord fight my battle, victory shall be mine" is full of wisdom.

Joseph has come to the end of his prison term without a lawyer, without an advocacy group to speak on his behalf, even without trying to defend himself. He came to the end of the term simply because God had a set time to bring him to his place of purpose and power. You must keep your hands in your pockets and take them out only to clap or raise them in praise, or to receive the blessings that God is going to place in them. Simply put, you can't fight with the tactics that your enemy is trying to fight you. When you are in a trial that is trying your very existence, it is the finest moment for you to say nothing. Every day that the calendar turns, it brings you closer to the day when God will reveal to those who stand around who have lied and who have told the truth. Truth is something that many people are not seeking, nor are they concerned about until it is them who need to be vindicated.

God is too righteous to leave us in our trial forever, his hand of mercy is outstretched to those who have called him from within their hearts. His strength is revealed in view that we have survived things that would have killed us had we been outside of his will. Joseph lived through his trial because he knew deep within himself that there was a reason for his existence. His name being called to come to the palace doesn't excite him, he is not running nor is he trying to escape. This moment is divine, this moment is the moment that what he has in him is going to be revealed, for nobody in all of Egypt has what he has, he has a God-given revelation of the coming season; no one has that. I want to say to you that what you have, no one has. That is the wonder-working power of the God that we serve; what he has given to each of us, he uniquely crafted within us. Which means you don't have to live in the shadow of someone else's time. Each of us will have our own defining moment, each of us will have the moment when our name is called to come into the place he has purposed us for. Is it your turn? If so, don't rush, don't gloat, just embrace the moment; "It's Your Turn, Take Your Time."

CHAPTER 8

"IT'S IN ME BUT IT'S NOT MINE"

One of my most prized possessions is the anointing that God has given unto me. It is precious, it is sacred, and even though it is in me, it is not mine. It is what God has given me to pour out upon situations and circumstances which are absent of his power and his presence. Therefore, because I am carrying it for God and for someone else, I must treat it as though it belongs to someone else and not myself. Though it seems hard and unfair, Joseph was carrying a preservation season for the very people who were trying to destroy him. There is a place in your story where it will be all about others and you will only be the pencil that's writing the story. No one gives credence or credit to the pencil that writes the story, the pencil is just that, "the pencil." The story is revealed through the pencil, but the story doesn't belong to the pencil, the story belongs to the one who is writing it, and to those who will draw strength from it.

When Joseph stepped before Pharaoh, he was likened unto a pencil in the hand of a skilled writer. God has the amazing ability to allow what is in you to become revelation knowledge to direct someone who is in the dark to see the light. Many times, we hold the key to someone living or dying; we hold the key to their failure and their success. Joseph, like a tool in the hands of a master carpenter is about to unveil the blueprint of his purpose to the entire world. Your purpose must be revealed in order for God to give you your next assignment. The purpose of Joseph being in Egypt was not to be a butler, a prisoner, or a slave. The purpose of Joseph being in Egypt was to be a deliverer from the coming season. Pharaoh's troublesome dreams were catalysts that would bring to light his purpose, but also it would bring to light God's ability to put something in someone else, that he may pull out what he has placed in another.

These troublesome dreams that Pharaoh had were dreams that couldn't be interpreted by anyone in his palace. It was set up by God that only the power of God was able to bring about the revelation of what he dreamed. When God uses you to be a light in a dark place; SHINE! The dreams of fat cows being eaten by skinny cows and big ears of corn being blasted by thin ears of corn were all troubling. Though they were troubling, they were not troubling to Joseph. He revealed to Pharaoh that what it meant was a famine was coming. There would be seven years of plenty, but the famine would be so grievous that it would make it seem as if the seven years of plenty never existed. Joseph admonished Pharaoh to appoint an overseer and store food during the time of plenty that when the time of famine arrived, they would have food in Egypt. Pharaoh said to him, "Who is wiser than you, you are the one who needs to oversee this task." That day, his name would change, that day he would get a wife, and that day he would arise to second in command to Pharaoh.

You are but one step from being used by God in a way that you never dreamed of, you are one step from the greatest elevations that you have ever experienced. There is someone looking for what's inside of you. The gift, the anointing, the revelation that you have, is in you, but it is for someone else. Without you pouring it out upon or in the life of someone else, it remains inside of you, but that is not why God gave it to you. Joseph has given to Pharaoh something that will cause lives to be preserved and a nation to be saved. To withhold what God has placed on the inside of you from others is to dishonor the God who gave it to you. I want my life to be a fragrance to those whom God has anointed me to help change their lives. I don't want to hold what I have been anointed to hand out, I don't want to keep what I have been charged to give away.

Many people have merchandised what God intended for them to give away. They have taken gifts which God has given them to share and bless others with and used them in the wrong manner. Joseph says to Pharaoh, does not all interpretations belong to God? He opened his mouth and began to reveal the mystery that was attached to Pharaoh's dreams. There is someone waiting for the light to come on in a dark place. Their survival depends upon someone coming in time to turn the light on so they can see. The question is, are you that person? Do you possess in your vessel the necessary element to bring someone out of what they thought they would die in? This is a critical time and a crucial moment!

Joseph didn't allow the bitterness of what had happened to him, to cause him to withhold his gift from the one who needed it. There are times that we suffer some of the most horrendous things and after we suffer, we withhold what God has placed in us from the very ones who need it most. Suffering has a way of turning us into something beautiful or turning us into something or someone we no longer recognize. The hurt, the many nights that we've cried and no one wiped our tears, the times people had what we needed and yet they withheld it from us, it will either make you bitter or better. I have seen it happen to the best of people. God trusts us with his most precious and powerful gifts. He trusts that when we see how good he has been to us, despite how mean and ugly people can be, we will remember his goodness, therefore we will stretch our hands to help another.

If there was anyone who had the right to be bitter and angry, it would have been Joseph, yet he never stopped to second guess at any time, should he or shouldn't he pour out what was in him. I want to end this segment by saying to you if you pour it out, you utilize your gift to its maximum capacity, but if you hold it, you waste it. There are many individuals who have wasted their gifts because they selectively withheld them from those who needed them the most. They chose where and when they would share what was on the inside of them, rather than allowing the opportunity to choose. Because Joseph did not allow his feelings and flesh to get in the way, he sets himself up for one of the greatest moments in his life. He is getting ready to see the goodness of the Lord in the land of the living.

Psalms 27:13 KJV I had fainted, unless I had believed to see the goodness of the Lord in the Land of the living....

GOD DOESN'T WASTE PAIN

Life can bring with it some of the most plaguing questions. Each and every setup, setback, and pitfall can leave you with things embedded in your mind that you have no answers for, nor do you have any answers to. It is like being dropped off in a strange place where you don't know the culture, nor do you speak the language. People are moving all about, however, you are unaware of what they are saying and what they are doing around you. Many times, we have been placed in situations that we don't understand what is going on around us. People whom we thought would make the journey with us turned into total strangers along the way. Places we thought we would remain for the duration of our lives have long ago become distant memories.

When you build a house and it is completed, if you look at all the materials and furnishings that went into it, you will discover that the materials have come from all over the world. Though it has come from all over the world, the beauty of the house speaks of how God can take many things from many places and make it a masterpiece. Designers specify how something can be useless when it's alone, and become valuable when it is added to something else. A piece of broken glass is useless alone. However, when you find someone who is masterful in making artifacts from broken glass, one broken piece added to another broken piece is precious. A broken relationship added to a broken promise can be heartbreaking. However, the providence of God can weld it together through someone else's testimony and it becomes powerful to another.

Joseph has endured unimaginable pain! He has survived what would have sent others into shock just thinking about it. However, he has not allowed the unimaginable to stifle his God-given gift. There are some things that are made to handle hard situations. It is made to handle difficult things, and the greater the difficulty, the better the performance. When we look at an Ox in the scriptures, it is an animal that was used to handle hard tasks. The harder the task, the more the Ox would pull. If the Ox couldn't complete the task, it would pull until its heart burst, because it would rather die than to not have pleased its Master. This should be the burning desire of every believer in Christ. I want to please my Master, and I will give my life trying to do so.

We look at pain as a reason to quit, if it hurts us, we back away and we sometimes leave the task undone. I have performed the task so many times with tears in my eyes and a heart that was broken, yet I finished the task that was at hand. Pain signifies you are in territory that is unfamiliar to what you are used to. Joseph was in a place he never thought he would be. He didn't understand why he was there. It didn't feel good to him, but God was about to make it all make sense. Simply put, "God Doesn't Waste Pain". There is no place in your life that he doesn't see nor does he not know that you are there, there is no incident that you have embarked upon that he doesn't know about.

The famine that God revealed to Pharaoh was a worldwide famine, which means it happened over the whole earth. There was no place on the earth that was not affected by the famine, therefore the famine was also in Israel. Everyone was seeking food; they went to whatever lengths to make sure that they had food for their families to eat. The word has come to every nation and tongue that there is food in Egypt, therefore all nations came down to buy food, for the famine was so grievous all over the world. Jacob, Joseph's father, has heard that there is food in Egypt and he says to his sons, there is food in Egypt, go and buy us some that we may live. God lives in the future, the past, and the present all at the same time. His divine hand arranges circumstances, changes outcomes, and brings to pass prophecies that were spoken eons before.

Joseph's brothers make their trek to Egypt to buy food. They come down with the intention of obtaining the food and taking it back to Israel, but what they don't know is they are about to have a close encounter with God's divine providence. There are people who mistreated you, misused you, and discounted you- who will sooner or later need you! God has shown Joseph something in one place that will take place a world away from the place he showed it to him. His brothers come to Egypt to receive food, yet they will see God's hand in such a way that they will never forget. Though this is divine in nature, it is yet painful. Because God is in it, doesn't mean it doesn't hurt, nor does it mean that you will not have all of the emotions that come along with being betrayed, it hurts just as much. However, what helps you to heal from the hurt you've experienced is that you know that you are in God's will.

Joseph is about to come full circle with the things which God has shown unto him in the visions which he had as a boy. The lies and the betrayal of his brothers were more than just a family quarrel spawned from jealousy and envy. It is about to be revealed that God has the ability to make someone hate you enough to place you in an uncomfortable place, all because he loves you and the perpetrator as well. Joseph's brothers are about to witness the unintentional elevation of their brother done by their hate and hands. Never underestimate God's power to use the hate and deceit of your enemies as a tool to push you into a prosperous season. The will of God is manifested in ways that the mind of man can never understand, nor the eyes of mankind can see it coming. Destiny knows every road, tunnel, pit, and sabotage in this world, and our God directs the entirety of it all.

The fact that Joseph's brothers needed the hands of the same man whom they threw in a pit and sold into slavery, says that what they did, pushed him into a place he never would've been, had it not been for their treachery. It was evil, but it was an anointed evil. It was heinous, but it was an anointed heinous action. The plan of God overrides the plots of every enemy attack. There is nothing that the enemy onslaughts can do to you that will prevail over the plans that God has for you. Lies, setups, and setbacks are sometimes used as the reason we should give God praise despite what we have gone through. After all they had done to Joseph, he was yet alive, not only alive, but he had arisen to a powerful position as being second in command to Pharaoh. God's will is sometimes for others to let you down so that he can lift you up. No, it doesn't sound good, nor does

ory that

we choose God's grace, mercy, and blessings over retribution. God
revealed his grace upon Joseph in such a way that his brothers didn't
even know who he was when they saw him. When he was thrown
in the pit years before he was a teenager, they were older than him.
However, at that age, his facial structure should have resembled
them in some way; after all, they were brothers. One thing I lift is
the fact that he knew them, but they didn't know him. The same
heart will cause you to be the same, but if the heart is different, it
will cause you to look different. Joseph had a different heart than his
brothers, therefore he looked different. On the other hand, they had
the same heart, and they still looked the same. He knew them, but
they didn't know him.

When he saw them, he had to remove himself from their
presence to cry. His weeping was so bitter that he asked every one

137

of his servants to leave him alone. Every ounce of pain that he felt or had ever experienced flooded his soul and his heart. Some of us have pain stored in our hearts and minds that have been there for so many years. Incident after incident that we've never healed from, and no one took the time to allow us to release it. So, we live day to day full of pain and heartaches, and every now and again we awake from a night's sleep, only to find tear tracks dried to our faces. We cry in the convenience of privacy, but we wear the hurt publicly hidden behind smiles and busy lives. But I need to tell you that God doesn't waste pain. He takes the pain that we experience and turns it into a totally different adverse reaction. Joseph's pain was turned into power-he didn't let the lies of Potiphar's wife make him bitter. He didn't let the butler's broken promise make him disavow his gift or put it away under an excuse. He maintained his integrity despite what others had done to him.

God will not let the pain we have experienced be wasted; he will not let it become hate that we use against those who hurt us. God doesn't waste pain! God weighs pain on the scale of elevation and he passes new levels to those who can handle the most pain without allowing it to change their hearts. This is someone's moment of elevation and it will come at the expense of the pain that you have gone through in your life. Just when you thought that God had overlooked what you have suffered or skipped over you for some reason or another, he comes back with a blessing for you, that's been paid for by everything that you have experienced. God doesn't waste pain……..

"THE CONFIRMATION IS WORTH MORE THAN THE CONFRONTATION"

The world is not big enough for us not to one day meet the people behind the attacks we have suffered. One day, perhaps on purpose or on happenstance, you will come face to face with the person or persons who are responsible for some of your most grievous trials. When they can't get you to respond to them through text, email, or phone, the last plot is to arrange for an unintentional face-to-face meeting. The plight of your enemy is that you will behave in a way that will destroy your character and act out in some way to shame you and redeem them. The Bible is a book of confirmation and confrontation. It is the very reason that we are saved. God has confronted Satan through Jesus about you and me. We are confirmation that Jesus defeated the devil in the pits of hell.

Joseph has come to the moment of confrontation. There are things that we have seen in dreams that God has confirmed to us by allowing them to manifest. Some of the things that we've seen, we didn't want to see, because it revealed to us the heart of someone that we never felt had ill will toward us. Then there are some things that we saw that we had no clue of what it meant because God used symbols instead of the faces of people. God will use symbols sometimes and not faces, because we may prematurely get rid of the person before they serve their purpose for being in our lives. Everyone will serve out their full sentence of purpose in our lives. It matters not who they are and where they live; no lawyer or District

Attorney can free them until they have served their sentence of purpose.

God revealed symbols to Joseph in his visions as a boy, and he also revealed to him numbers, however, he did not reveal to him faces. God is the God of divine revelation and he is the God of time and circumstance. The heart is built to withstand some of the most painful circumstances, yet our emotions are not built to handle what our heart can stand. His emotional breakdown revealed that what happened to him hurt him, though he showed no signs of it while he was going through it. This is significant because emotions are built to respond to events and the circumstances we go through. It's the body's normal way to survive the things that hurt us the deepest. Our emotions are our safeguards. He cried with such anguish that he was heard all over the palace. There are people that have hurt you and me and they don't have a clue of the depth of the hurt. Everyone who says they are alright is not alright, everyone who says that they are not hurt isn't telling the truth.

Sometimes, the only thing that keeps us alive in what we have been thrust into is what God has revealed to us before we began our journey. That's the motivating mechanism, which for many, it has kept them breathing, it has kept them expecting. The sabotage of his brothers, the lies that were told on him by this evil woman to cause him to be thrust into prison. All of this was embedded in his emotions. It is the last gate that he has to come through before fulfillment is revealed. It is the moment in which he has to reveal himself to the ones who caused him to be sold and imprisoned.

Sometimes, the hardest thing to do is confront the source of your sabotage. Sometimes, the hardest thing to do is to confront the man behind the mask. Confrontation can send you into shock! Even though it hurts to finally see the face behind the mask, it is a relief, you have to give God praise, and thank him that he would not allow you to live in the dark all of your life.

Genesis 42:6-9 KJV

And Joseph was the governor over the land and he it was that sold to all the people of the land: and Joseph's brethren, came, and bowed down themselves before him with their faces to the earth.

And Joseph saw his brethren, and he knew them, but made himself strange unto them, and spake roughly unto them; and he said unto them whence come ye? And they said, From the Land of Canaan to buy food.

And Joseph knew his brethren, but they knew not him.

And Joseph remembered the dreams which he dreamed of them, and said unto them, Ye are spies; to see the nakedness of the land you have come...

What God has said to us and what God has shown us stands paramount over what people have done to us. There is nothing that anyone can do to me that will not come along with a Word Reference from God. God will refer you through the Holy Ghost back to what he has already said to you when an attack arises against you. You must conquer and master your emotions that you do not break down, before you breakthrough. This is key because to be able to compose yourself in the face of those who are behind your greatest pain reveals that *the confirmation is worth more than the confrontation.* The fact that I know that everything that has happened in this entire situation was under God's orchestration says to me that I must be some kind of special if God trusted me to keep this secret for this long.

If you notice Joseph never told the story of how he got to Egypt-he never told the story that he knew who put him in the pit. However, he knew who did it, and he knew why they did it, yet he never said anything to any of the Egyptians about it. Neither would he tell any of them anything about it afterward. Child of God, that is powerful! That I don't have to tell my side of the story while I'm going through it and I don't have to tell it when I come through it, because the confirmation is worth more than the confrontation. He fed them and gave them provision for their animals, knowing all the time that it was them who were behind his suffering. Your act of kindness toward the one who has done you the greatest evil destroys the seed that sabotage can leave in us. Confirmation gives you the assurance that you have conquered the challenges and mastered the changes you've had to go through. Now you have moved into the place where God intended for you to be; that is the place of peace.

It is so mind-blowing that those who are around us do not understand why we are not torn apart viewing the challenges and changes that we go through. God has so many ways to groom us and grow us to be what he wants us to be. Joseph's brothers are not hostile toward him this time like they were the last time that he saw them. Perhaps they don't know him, perhaps another view of that would be because they needed him. Need sometimes takes the face-off of people and it sometimes makes them forget everything that they have done prior to them arriving at the point of need. The record which God keeps is an immaculate one. It doesn't have any flaws, nor are there any incorrect instances or incidents. He doesn't forget, he passes out points and favors to all in hope that they will turn to him and be saved.

Joseph spent some time toying with his brothers-making them question themselves to the point that they believed that an omen had befallen them because of what they had done to their brother, many years ago. The satisfaction of confirmation and the ability that God has to make your enemy remember what they have done to you is repayment enough. Many people inwardly want others to suffer for what they have done to them. There is no need to wish for evil upon another when it comes to God, he handles every evil and elevation accordingly. The long road back and forth to Canaan from Egypt with this man on their mind who seemed to know everything about them and their father was almost horrifying. It shifted from horrifying to the blame game. The very thought of someone that they had put in a hole and sold like an animal at an auction, who had somehow survived and arisen to power made them shake in their shoes.

God will make every individual, whether righteous or wicked, acknowledge his mighty works and his mighty hand of power. You cannot get around the God who makes all things work according to the counsel of his own divine will. No one can elevate themselves and expect God to favor them in a place he never called them to be. Neither can any person usurp authority over another that God has favored, and place them in a place of a lower degree because of their dislike for God's choice. Simply put, we must leave God's business in God's hands. There is no room for man's hand in God's business when it deals with his favor and elevation. He opens doors and closes them when he gets ready for whomever he will. Josephs' brothers learned that you can't kill prophecy, nor can you sell off visionaries for dollars and cents.

Joseph is alive and, might I add, very much alive. After he had put his brothers through many quests and asked them many questions, Joseph finally revealed to them who he was. It was emotionally revealing, yet it was absent of blame and it was absent of anger. The one way that you know you have purpose over pain that God has given you a divine assignment is regardless of who is behind it all, the emotion of gratitude overcomes the emotion of anger. Every attack you have suffered makes sense when every step of your journey has been made. Your journey makes no sense without the revelation of confirmation. There must be a defining moment when everything that you have dreamed, envisioned, and suffered will all make sense. Until then, those around you will figure that you are just someone trying to rise to a place of authority, just as Joseph's brothers felt about him. What I love about God is his ability to bring every attack, everyone behind the attack, every naysayer, and the one it has been against, into one place; that one place is confirmation.

Confirmation answers all questions reveals all intents and opens all eyes. Whether they want to be open or not, whether they believe what they see or not, God will reveal who he has his hands upon. The question becomes at what juncture do you believe what you see over what someone said. At what interval of time do you accept God's sovereign will over the wishes and whims of someone who has an agenda that matches their dislike of God's choice? Regardless of how you feel Joseph, you are the choice and you will get the chance for your haters to fall in your hands. However, *you must exemplify Kingdom Character in a volatile moment.*

ANOINTED LIES

The wonderful works of God have encased in them the evil intent of mankind. There are no roadblocks, pits, people, persecutions, nor anything else that can prevent God's will from being revealed through and to his people. The age-old weaponry of lies and twisted truths are not powerful enough to prevent the eternality of God's Triune existence. Lies are used as Satan's ready weapons, they are his go-to arsenal. They have the ability to destroy lives, get people killed, and in some cases get others promoted, yet they don't work according to their intent in some places as good as they do in others. There have been many individuals who have maintained innocence their whole prison term, only to find out 50 years later that they were telling the truth the whole time. Lies, lies, lies, the enemies' number one weapon and roadblocks are lies.

145

When we read the Bible, we find there are many incidents where a lie was the enemy's weapon of choice, yet it was powerless in the end. The God of all power has access to all things that have power, even if they are negative. This tells us that what the enemy uses as an evil weapon of power, God has power over that as well. How disappointing it must be to try and use a weapon on someone and the weapon ends up empowering the one it was intended to be used on. The message of this entire Holy Writ that we read is filled with plots and the plans of enemy infiltration through lies and the fragile power of false matrixes. Any weapon, matters not how powerful one thinks it is, will lose its intended power in the presence of the God of all power. *Isaiah 54:17 KJV* *"No weapon that is formed against you shall be able to prosper and every tongue that rises against you shall be condemned for this is the heritage of the Lord, and their righteousness is of me saith the Lord of Host."*

The most powerful thing that we can conclude after it is all said and done is that God guides and guards. He guides those things that are sent out as weapons against his children and he guards us through every attack that we face. If the statement that I made is not true, I wouldn't be writing this work for you to read. Jesus, our supreme example, reveals to us that the moment the enemy detects that you have purpose and power, he will arrange for your demise. Joseph's attacks were covered by lies, which his brothers told to his father Jacob after they had thrown him in the pit. Jesus' attacks came through the lies that the Chief Priest and all that were against him formulated before he was crucified. The intention of the enemy is to shift the outcome of one's life with lies and falsities. It is the oldest weapon in Satan's arsenal. It is the easiest thing that he can do to try and stop, block or lock someone out of doors.

Even after the enemy has done all that he can, he yet doesn't possess the ability to stop the God who intercepts what he throws and yet make it work out for good. When we look at *Acts 6:8-15 KJV* , how a council of liars stacked a court of liars and had Stephen stoned to death, yet it didn't stop the work of God from coming to pass. There are many incidences in the Scriptures where lies were told to take the life of another, but God always brought retribution or vindication to avenge the individual's demise. We are assured that whatever happens to us, the God who sees all things will be both judge and jury to bring judgement upon those who destroy the life of another.

The revelation of maturity revealed to Joseph that despite the toils and the snares which he had gone through at the hands of his siblings, God had a plan that was greater than his pain and also it was greater than his brother's treachery. No lie has the power to stop the plan of God from manifesting in the life of those who he has purposed for power. There is no poison that can avert the destiny of God's choice. There is no individual who can gather enough ammunition to subvert the will of God from coming to pass, yet it doesn't stop people from trying to do so. One of the things that intrigues us is that we have sometimes been in situations where it looked as if we would die without a testimony, yet God used what was against us and turned it for our good.

Joseph wasn't angry in regards to what happened to him, from Canaan to Egypt. However, he was fulfilled in his understanding in regards to why it had to happen. There are some things that only make sense to us after we have received the entire revelation. Lies have a ministry when they are told against the children of God, yet the liar has a judgment to face because of the lies they have told. The ministry of a lie is to sometimes reveal the hand of evil, also to reveal the plan of elevation to us. There is nobody who has ever been lied on that would say I want to order another round of lies please. The reason being is because when we are defamed, it doesn't feel good to be shamed while people stand around and whisper about us. However, the more the enemy does this to us and we survive it and we come through it in favor, we then discover that lies have a ministry. The ministry of lies has navigated some people into places where they would never have ended up had it not been for the falsity.

Joseph revealed himself to his brothers to show them that what they did to him was a preplanned evil with malice and forethought. However, what God had done for him was also with intent and forethought. However, it was for a different reason. The anointing is God's charisma smeared on someone. It is God's favor painted upon someone. The question has to be, who can undo what God has done? I would readily answer that and say no, not one! Joseph was the recipient of a series of anointed lies, lie after lie that was intended to destroy him, but because God's favor was upon him, it would not happen. When you don't die at the wish of others, it kills them in some way. In the case of Joseph's brothers, they died to their evil when they saw the presence of God's favor upon him. They were astonished that he had survived what had happened to him. There are some people who are just as astonished when they see you after you have survived every attack. There was no way he was supposed to live through what had happened! Oh; there is a way, and that way is the Amazing Grace of God!

Lies land where they are supposed to, they are told with the purpose in which they are spread. Yet it doesn't annul the anointing; thus, when they are told, they become anointed lies. It is important that the bottom of the pit be touched by the hand of them that God will take to the top. It is a testament that God will sometimes let people put you down only for you to rise above the attack, while waving your hand with the dirt on it, as proof you've arisen from the bottom of the pit. Joseph had the whole story in chronological order. He had the story part by part, plot, storyline, and intrigue, but he also had the ending. The ending that no one saw but God, for it was God who showed him the end of the story from the beginning. *The Doctrine of Final Ends* is when God stands at the end of something, looking at the beginning. This was his case in Joseph's life, God saw the end of the story! That is what keeps us alive sometimes in firepits and snake-pits; God saw the end of the story.

Genesis 50:20 KJV "But as for you, ye thought evil against me; but God meant it unto Good, to bring to pass, as it is this day, to save much people alive.

The purpose of God is not just to save one person, the purpose of God is to save many people alive. His purpose is to take one individual and turn the entire story into a phenomenal outcome as if the story is a fictional account. The fact that lies were told on him was true, the fact that he had been thrown in a pit was true. The fact that Potiphar's wife lied on him and said he tried to rape her that was true. The fact that the butler lied and said he would remember him and he didn't'; all of it was true. However, every lie was anointed to bring him to his place to be a deliverer for God's people. Just like Joseph, God will get some glory out of your story and others will get some strength from your struggle. It will not be without pain; you'll have days that you will feel that God could have done it another way. Sometimes God goes along with the plan of the wicked that he might bring us out in a way that the wicked have to back up and look at us in amazement.

The trial that led Jesus to be crucified was riddled with lies and deceit. The Chief Priest and the Council hired liars to say that Jesus said he was going to destroy the Kingdom of Caesar. They stacked the courts with one witness after another to make sure that their accounts matched in order that their case wouldn't fall apart against Jesus. Though they arranged it in that fashion, it was divinely orchestrated, and God was the conductor. Jesus went to Calvary because of anointed lies. What they said about him was not true, yet it was God's will for them to say what they said. I have learned to let my enemies have their say. However, they won't have the last say. God moves us into position sometimes by the accusations of those who have ill will against us.

James 3:8 KJV "But the tongue can no man tame; it is an unruly evil, full of deadly poison."

I am far from insensitive when it comes to the hurt that comes along with being defamed and scandalized. One of the worst feelings is to work your whole life to build character and a good reputation then someone comes along with a lie to destroy it. Yet, when we look at what happened to Jesus, we see a different effect. How could someone be defamed and lied on, on the level in which he was defamed, and rise to be Savior of the whole world, and the most talked-about Man ever? The answer screams back that every liar was anointed to say what they said and every lie they told was anointed to get him to Calvary. We look at the word anointed, and we think it only ascertains to good and holy things, when the truth is every attack that pushes us toward purpose, is anointed. The lies that pushed Jesus to Calvary were anointed lies. Without lies, he would never have been crucified and without him being crucified, we would never have been saved. Whatever you are dealing with, regardless of how it started, who started it, realize that it is anointed to bring you into purpose and power. It's anointed to do its job, and you are anointed to live through it.

I Corinthians 2:8 KJV "*Because if they had known they would not have crucified the Lord of Glory."*